HOW TO THINK LIKE
BILL GATES

By the same author:

How to Think Like Sherlock
How to Think Like Steve Jobs
How to Think Like Mandela
How to Think Like Einstein
How to Think Like Churchill

HOW TO THINK LIKE
BILL GATES

DANIEL SMITH

Michael O'Mara Books Limited

For Mum

First published in Great Britain in 2015 by
Michael O'Mara Books Limited
9 Lion Yard
Tremadoc Road
London SW4 7NQ

A CIP catalogue record for this book is available from the British Library.

Papers used by Michael O'Mara Books Limited are natural,
recyclable products made from wood grown in sustainable forests.
The manufacturing processes conform to the environmental
regulations of the country of origin.

ISBN: 978-1-78243-373-6 in hardback print format
ISBN: 978-1-78243-375-0 in paperback print format
ISBN: 978-1-78243-374-3 in e-book format

1 3 5 7 9 10 8 6 4 2

Designed and typeset by Envy Design Ltd

Printed and bound by CPI Group (UK) Ltd, Croydon, CR0 4YY

www.mombooks.com

Contents

Introduction

'He had both the technical smarts to understand what's just around the corner, and the commercial smarts to sell it to the rest of us. This combination of talents makes Bill Gates one of a very rare breed of entrepreneurs.'

DES DEARLOVE, 1999

Bill Gates is many things to many people. To some he is an IT genius whose software has powered global business for over three decades. To others, he is the geek who conquered the world. His detractors see instead an icon of capitalist excess – a man who became the richest individual in the world before he was forty. Then, in the past few years and perhaps against expectations, Gates has been held up as the ultimate 'do-gooder', helping to redefine philanthropy for the modern age.

His is an extraordinary CV that reveals a man of great complexity. Born into a comfortable middle-class American family, it was soon evident that he was something of a prodigy when it came to computers. The first decades of his life were engaged in the insular business of writing code and developing his business empire. By the 1980s he had turned his company, Microsoft, into one of the most successful firms on the planet. He was one of the two great behemoths of the technological age, but where his great rival (and sometimes friend), Steve Jobs, brought an air of bohemian rebellion to the computer business, the bespectacled Gates came to be a figurehead of the staid but booming corporate America.

As a businessman, he garnered a reputation for ruthlessness. He not only knew how to develop a product for market, but he was great at selling it there, too. Indeed, some have accused him of being overly concerned with getting one over on his business rivals, accusations that led to years of litigation over the legitimacy of a few of Microsoft's business practices. Such has been the dominance of Gates-originated software driving the world's PCs that other developers have understandably felt there has been little room left for them. Gates in turn argued that Microsoft merely reaped the rewards for being great innovators.

Having started his business out of his bedroom, Gates found himself transformed from the plucky little guy that people liked to back to the head of a global empire that many had come to loathe. Once your personal wealth dwarfs the GDP of most of the world's countries, it is difficult to cast yourself as a 'man of the people'. Although hugely intelligent and articulate, Gates also lacks that natural charisma that won Jobs pop star-like popularity even as the billions rolled into his bank account.

By the mid-1990s, though, it was evident that Gates was changing. The nerdy techie guy who spent days and nights at a time refining computer software was entering middle age. He married and had kids and, crucially, turned away from his monitor to look out at the world. The injustices he saw shocked and appalled him. That your chances of a good education and even a decently long life are so intrinsically linked to the lottery of where you happen to be born came as a revelation.

Having spent the first few decades of his life capitalizing on his talents to make himself absurdly rich, he decided it was time to give something back. In a gradual process, he stepped away from the day-to-day running of Microsoft and put his energies instead into philanthropy. Nor did his wish to improve the world prove to be a passing fad. The Bill and Melinda Gates Foundation, which he established in 2000 with his wife, is now one of the richest charitable organizations in the world. Perhaps even more importantly, the way it operates is heavily influencing how the sector as a whole goes about its business.

Naturally, not everyone is a fan of the ways the foundation generates capital or how it disperses it – Gates himself acknowledges that not all of its operations have achieved what he desired. But few argue that it hasn't had an enormous impact, both within the USA and in the wider developing world. If, as many expect, polio is wiped out as a killer disease within the next few years, the Gates Foundation must be given a great deal of credit for its part in the fight.

Gates, then, has entirely reinvented himself. A man who for many represented the 'take, take, take' culture of Western capitalism in the 1980s and 1990s has become the leading figure of the 'give, give, give' movement in the twenty-first century. *Time* magazine named him one of the 100 people who most influenced the twentieth century. Now we struggle to know whether his greatest legacy will be his contribution to the development of computing or his reconfiguration of what we think of as charity.

How to Think Like Bill Gates is designed to take a look at key aspects of his character and ideology, as well as to consider some of the most important influences on him at the different stages of his life. If the *How to Think Like* series proves anything, it is that great figures are rarely straightforward, and Gates is no less nuanced than any of the other subjects covered. He is a man of prodigious talent, pugnacious in his business dealings and sometimes, necessarily, ruthless. He is at heart a problem-solver (whether it be how to make a spreadsheet work better or how to reduce global poverty) who in his early years was driven in no small part by a desire for personal recognition and material gain. The older Gates, though, is less interested in accumulating personal wealth than in figuring out how to best make use of it. That transition is a fascinating one and each chapter of his life offers lessons of enduring relevance.

Landmarks in a
Remarkable Life

1955   William Henry Gates III is born on 28 October to William and Mary Gates in Seattle,
Washington. He becomes known as Trey by his
family and as Bill to the wider world.

1967   Bill begins attending an exclusive private
preparatory school, Lakeside, in the Haller
Lake neighbourhood of north Seattle.

1968   A member of the school's computing club,
he writes his first program, using the BASIC
language on a Teletype Model 33 terminal
linked to a remote mainframe computer. A
fellow club member is Paul Allen, with whom
Gates will eventually found Microsoft.

1970   Gates and Allen write a traffic-surveillance
program that they call Traf-O-Data, which
earns the teenagers several thousand dollars.

1972   Gates works as a congressional page (an assistant to a member) in the US House of Representatives for the summer.

1973   After acing his high-school SATs, Gates enrols on Harvard's pre-law programme. There he befriends Steve Ballmer.

1974   Gates and Allen spend the summer working for Honeywell, a New Jersey-based technology company.

1975   Gates and Allen produce a BASIC software package for the Altair 8800, a landmark personal computer produced by MITS. Gates drops out of Harvard to join Allen in Albuquerque, New Mexico, in order to work for the company. The two co-found Micro-soft.

1976   Microsoft (as it is now known) is formally registered as a company. Gates publishes an open letter condemning software theft by computer hobbyists.

1977   The relationship with MITS breaks down over commercial disagreements. Meanwhile, Gates is introduced to Kazuhiko Nishi, who helps launch Microsoft in Japan.

1978   The company opens a Japanese sales office. Microsoft's revenues top US$1 million for the year.

1979   The company relocates its US base to Gates and Allen's hometown, Seattle.

Landmarks in a Remarkable Life

1980   Microsoft agrees to provide an operating system for the personal computer being developed by industry giants, IBM.

1981   Microsoft is incorporated, with Gates assuming the posts of CEO and chairman. He takes a 53% stake in the company. Steve Jobs, boss of Apple, approaches Gates about designing software for the imminent Apple Macintosh.

1983   *Time* names the computer as its Machine of the Year. Paul Allen leaves Microsoft, having been diagnosed with Hodgkin's disease.

1985   Microsoft launches its Windows operating system, which employs a graphical user interface.

1986   Microsoft goes public. Gates's shareholding is valued at hundreds of millions of dollars.

1987   Gates becomes the youngest billionaire in history. At an event in New York, he meets Melinda French, an employee who will become his wife.

1988   Apple unsuccessfully sues Microsoft, with Jobs accusing Gates of plundering Macintosh innovations in the creation of Windows.

1989   Gates establishes the Corbis digital image archive. Microsoft launches Office, a suite of applications including Word and Excel.

1990   Buoyed by the release of Windows 3.0, company revenues top $1 billion for the first time.

1992	Gates is named by *Forbes* as the richest person in the United States.
1993	The Department of Justice begins investigating Microsoft for anti-trust practices.
1994	Gates marries Melinda French. He also founds the William H. Gates Foundation.
1995	Windows 95 launches, along with Microsoft's own web browser, Internet Explorer. Gates releases his first book, *The Road Ahead*. *Forbes* names him the richest person in the world for the first time, with a fortune just short of $13 billion.
1996	Melinda Gates gives birth to a daughter, Jennifer. Netscape, an internet browser company, requests the Department of Justice investigate the bundling of Windows and Internet Explorer.
1997	Gates and his family move into their custom-built Lake Washington estate.
1998	The Department of Justice charges Microsoft with anti-competitive practices.
1999	Melinda gives birth to a son, Rory. Gates publishes a second book, *Business @ the Speed of Thought*. Microsoft stock reaches an all-time high.
2000	Gates is replaced as Microsoft CEO by his old college friend, Steve Ballmer. Gates takes the title Chief Software Architect. A judge rules the company should be split in two – one part

dealing with the Windows operating system, and another part with all other software. The decision is overturned a year later. Meanwhile, the William H. Gates Foundation is subsumed into the newly established Bill and Melinda Gates Foundation.

2001   Windows XP is launched, as is the Xbox games console.

2002   Melinda gives birth to another daughter, Phoebe.

2004   The European Commission launches an anti-trust case against Microsoft.

2005   *Time* names Bill and Melinda Gates as its Persons of the Year, alongside Bono, in recognition of their philanthropic work. Bill also receives an honorary knighthood from the UK.

2006   Billionaire investor Warren Buffett commits the majority of his wealth to the Bill and Melinda Gates Foundation. Microsoft announce that Gates will end his full-time role with the company in 2008.

2007   Microsoft launches Windows Vista. Gates receives an honorary degree from Harvard, thirty-two years after dropping out.

2008   The European Commission imposes a record fine of $1.4 billion on Microsoft. Gates leaves his full-time position as scheduled in June to devote more time to his foundation. At a meeting of the World Economic Forum in Davos, he introduces his philosophy of 'creative capitalism'.

2010   The foundation pledges $10 billion over ten years to help research, develop, and deliver vaccines for the world's poorest countries.

2011   The foundation launches the 'Reinvent the Toilet Challenge', an initiative to encourage innovation in the interests of the 2.5 billion people without access to safe sanitation.

2012   Polio is declared no longer endemic to India, a milestone in Gates's mission to rid the world of the disease.

2013   The Gates Foundation links up with the Bill, Hillary & Chelsea Clinton Foundation to assess the progress of women and girls around the world.

2014   Gates leaves his role as Microsoft chairman. He agrees to become a special adviser to new company CEO, Satya Nadella. He is also once again named by *Forbes* as the world's richest person, after a hiatus from the top spot dating back to 2010.

2015   An opinion poll conducted for *The Times* newspaper finds Gates is the most admired person in the world.

Engage
Your Brain

'Life's a lot more fun if you treat its
challenges in creative ways.'

BILL GATES IN INTERVIEW
WITH AUTHOR JANET LOWE, 1998

No one can say that Bill Gates's story is one of rags to riches. There was no need for him to fight his way out of the ghetto or pull himself up by his bootstraps. Nonetheless, his early life is an object lesson in making the most of the advantages bestowed upon you.

William Henry Gates III was born in Seattle, Washington state, on 28 October 1955. His parents were William Gates, Sr, a lawyer, and Mary, a teacher and businesswoman, and Bill would be their middle child and only son. The family was keen on card games and so Bill came to be known as Trey, a card-player's term for a 'Three' that reflected his 'III' designation.

Both parents were thoughtful and well educated, and wished the same for their offspring. From his youngest days, Bill was encouraged to occupy himself with interests that would stretch the mind. So, for instance, television was banned on school nights – a rule with which Gates was relatively easily reconciled. As he would tell an interviewer in 1986, 'I'm not one of those people who hates TV, but I don't think it exercises your mind much.' Instead of being glued to the screen, the Gates family instead indulged their passion for, among other pastimes, conversation, games and reading.

This latter activity fundamentally moulded Gates's life through its many and varied phases, and we shall look at his relationship with books in more depth later (see 'Read Like Bill Gates', page 142). Meanwhile, family discussions on everything from current affairs to culture, sport and the trivia of everyday life ensured that the young Bill had a broad base of interests and the ability to articulate his opinions. Contrary to the popular image of the average trailblazing techno-geek, Bill was never the introverted little boy who found comfort behind the protection of a computer screen.

In fact, he was something of an extrovert, and a highly competitive one at that. As might be expected in a family that awarded him a nickname related to card playing, the Gates clan encouraged competitiveness. As an example, each year the family holidayed in an area by the Hood Canal, near Puget Sound. The Gateses would go with several other young families and the highlight of the vacation was always a mini-Olympics in which they all competed. Although Bill was quite a small physical specimen, he was doughty and determined. Only the foolhardy underestimated him as an opponent. Speaking to author Janet Lowe in 1998, he revealed, 'In the summer, we'd … play a lot of competitive games – relay races, egg tosses, Capture the Flag. It was always a great time, and it gave all of us a sense that we could compete and succeed.'

In retrospect, it should come as little surprise that Bill was particularly keen on games of strategy, especially chess (in which he desired to be a Grandmaster) and 'Go'. His performance benefitted from his natural grasp of logic and a seriously impressive memory. On one occasion, the minister at the family church offered a prize to anyone who could learn the Sermon on the Mount off by heart. Gates was, of course, word perfect when he came to deliver it. His youthfully exuberant explanation when the minister asked how he had managed such a feat: 'I can do any-thing I set my mind to.'

His ability to memorize is further evidenced by the fact that well into adulthood he was able to reel off his lines from a high-school play in which he appeared. Such perfect recall proved most useful as his passion for computer programming grew, with his ability to remember great expanses of computer code putting him ahead of the game.

Growing up in an era of *Boys' Own*-tales of space exploration, Gates was also open to the technological possibilities of the future. When he was six, he visited the world's fair in Seattle, the centrepiece of which was an awesomely tall observation tower known as the Space Needle. In America in the early 1960s, the future was a place in which everything was possible and he bought into the idea wholeheartedly. In Gates's case, the boy really was the father of the man, as it is a dream that he has never let go of.

Gates showed promise in his early years at school but his attention was prone to wander, so in sixth grade (around the age of eleven) his parents moved him to a private school, Lakeside, where they hoped he would be given work to challenge his burgeoning intellect. He demonstrated particular potential in the areas of mathematics and science – when he took his SATs in 1973 he scored a perfect 800 on the maths component. Not that he was a one-trick pony, though: he continued to nurture a broad range of interests, showing a liking for drama and politics in his senior years. Many years later he would acknowledge that his teens were pivotal in his development, declaring to Steven Levy, author of *Hackers: Heroes of the Computer Revolution*, that his 'software mind' was shaped by the time he was seventeen.

Others were quick to see his promise. Several Ivy League universities came calling and he chose Harvard. However, like his great rival-to-be, Steve Jobs, he skipped a lot of classes once he was in college.

He continued to excel in those subjects that interested him but simply disengaged with those that did not. He did, though, make full use of the computer labs, undertaking his own projects and sometimes spending days at a time there. And when he got bored, he filled his hours with poker marathons.

Gates was born into an environment where lively intellect was not only admired but actively encouraged. Quick-witted, thoughtful and excited by what the world had to offer, he thrived. He may not have been the model student – especially in those areas that captured his imagination less – but he embraced his own intelligence and never felt the need, as so many children do, to hide it from the world.

In a 2000 book by Cynthia Crossen, *The Rich and How They Got That Way*, Gates is quoted as saying: 'Smartness is an ability to absorb new facts. To ask an insightful question. To absorb it in real time. A capacity to remember. To relate to domains that may not seem connected at first.' It is a credo that has served him well.

Gates's Heroes

'How can an ugly little guy who isn't even really
French manage to rise up and rewrite the
laws of Europe … This is one smart guy.'

BILL GATES, QUOTED IN *GATES: HOW MICROSOFT'S
MOGUL REINVENTED AN INDUSTRY — AND MADE
HIMSELF THE RICHEST MAN IN AMERICA* (1993)

Gates was never one for hero-worship, even as a teen, when most of us adorn our walls with images of sportspeople, pop stars, movie icons or political revolutionaries, to whom our devotion may or may not stand the test of time. Nonetheless, he developed a small coterie of figures whom he admired, including some of the greatest figures in history.

He was, for instance, a great fan of Sir Isaac Newton, the seventeenth- to eighteenth-century natural philosopher best remembered for his formulation of the laws of gravity. As a fellow mathematician and physicist, Gates of course aspired only to the very best. Also deemed worthy of his adulation was Leonardo da Vinci, the Italian polymath whose varied achievements (from painting the *Mona Lisa* to designing a prototype flying machine centuries before human flight was achieved) made him the archetypal 'Renaissance Man'. Leonardo has continued to cast a spell on Gates into adulthood, and an expensive one at that, as we shall see in the chapter 'Enjoy the Trappings of Your Success' (page 126). As he said in *The New York Times* in 1995: 'Leonardo was one of the most amazing people who ever lived. He was a genius in more fields than any scientist of any age, and an astounding painter and sculptor.'

LEADERS OF MEN

It is telling that one historical character to have piqued Gates's fascination was Napoleon Bonaparte, the great French general-turned-dictator. Both relatively diminutive of stature, they each set out to conquer the world through a mix of cool calculation and audacity. They mastered the skill of sniffing out the weaknesses of their rivals too, and earned reputations for a sometimes abrasive leadership style. It does not take much to reimagine Gates as the Napoleon of the technological age.

Other 'heroes' came on to the Gates radar later in life, although it has not been easy to meet his exacting criteria. Henry Ford, for example, failed to make the grade, serving as a role model when it came to attaining success but letting him down by his relative failure to retain it. Nelson Mandela, by contrast, won Gates's admiration for his almost unworldly magnanimity and his ability to maintain a cool rationale even in the face of extreme provocation. While parallels between the great anti-apartheid leader and the software wizard might have been hard to discern in Gates's younger days, it is much easier to see the influence of Mandela in his reincarnation as a global philanthropist.

Perhaps a more obvious subject of esteem for the early period Gates was Tiger Woods, who came from nowhere to set new standards in the golfing world not long after Gates had made a similar impact on the computing industry. Both achieved much while still very young and brought a focus to their respective fields that few others, if any, have matched.

Gates turned his attention to the modern scientific community for another favourite – the physics Nobel laureate, Richard Feynman. He was crestfallen when Feynman died in 1988, shortly after Gates had determined to meet him in person. Born in 1918, Feynman was an American theoretical physicist best known for his work in quantum mechanics (including quantum computing) and particle physics, and shared the 1965 Nobel Prize in Physics for his efforts in quantum electrodynamics. He also sought out innovative ways to present his discoveries, creating a pictorial system that came to be known as Feynman diagrams. Gates no doubt appreciated his grasp of the importance of both substance and style. But perhaps his appeal to the Microsoft supremo is best summed up in a couple of lines Feynman once wrote to one of his students: 'The worthwhile problems are the ones you can really solve or help solve, the ones you can really contribute something to … No problem is too small or too trivial if we can really do something about it.' They are words that could easily have tumbled from Gates's own mouth.

FRIEND AND ROLE MODEL

> 'Don't compare yourself with anyone in the world. If you do so, you are insulting yourself.'
>
> BILL GATES

Arguably the person who Gates most looks up to is a man who by his own admission has little feel for the technological world that Gates inhabits. Warren Buffett, however, is a fellow self-made multi-billionaire and one of Gate's chief rivals to the title of richest man in the world. He has also exerted enormous influence on Gates's philanthropic adventures. Born in Omaha, Nebraska, in 1930, Buffett is the head of Berkshire Hathaway and widely regarded as among the most wily investors who has ever lived. His fortune, which was estimated at $73 billion in 2015, came virtually exclusively from his knack of backing the right commercial horse. Known as the 'Oracle of Omaha', Buffett credits much of his success to following the principles espoused by the professional investor Benjamin Graham, whose works Buffett began studying in the late 1940s. To give an idea of Buffett's skills in making money out of money, a $10,000 investment in Berkshire Hathaway in 1965 was worth in excess of $50 million in 2014.

Gates met Buffett for the first time in 1991 at an event arranged by Bill's mother, Mary. They instantly hit it off. In 2006, the *Guardian* newspaper quoted Gates as saying Buffett 'has this very refreshing, simple way of looking at things'. It helped that they shared a sense of humour and the same broad political affiliations – both tend toward the Democratic party. They even have similar taste in food: despite their vast wealth and their regular attendance at grand banquets, both still enjoy the humble hamburger. Both also have an instinct for frugality so that on one occasion when the pair had travelled to China together, they opted to eat at a McDonald's and Buffett paid for the meal using money-off vouchers that he had made a point of carrying with him. Buffett's influence on his young protégé extends much further, though.

He was, for instance, responsible for Gates taking up the game of bridge with some seriousness. (For a man who had long enjoyed playing games, it is somewhat surprising that he had not come to bridge – the tactician's ultimate card game – earlier.) More significantly, Gates credits Buffett with fundamentally influencing the way he approaches commerce. In a speech at San Jose University in 1998, he said, 'I think Warren has had more effect on the way I think about my business and the way I think about running it than any business leader.' Buffett himself notably did not put his money in Microsoft but only because he makes it a rule to only invest in sectors he is confident he understands. The computer business does not fit that bill. He has, though, freely acknowledged Gates's entrepreneurial flair, saying in 1992, 'I'm not competent to judge his technical ability, but I regard his business savvy as extraordinary.'

However, surely posterity will regard Buffett's impact on Gates's philanthropy – in terms of financial backing, strategy formulation and moral support – as the most important fruit of their friendship (see page 166). In 2008, Gates said on the *Charlie Rose* show:

> Warren Buffet is the closest thing I have to a role model because of the integrity and thoughtfulness and joy he brings to everything he does. I'm continuing to learn from my dad, I'm continuing to learn from Warren and many times when I'm making decisions, I try and model how they'd approach a problem.

Find Your
True Calling

'I was lucky enough, at a young age, to discover
something that I loved and that fascinated
me – and still fascinates me.'

BILL GATES IN *INDUSTRY WEEK*, 1996

In 1986, a feature in the *Wall Street Journal* painted a picture of Bill Gates's life as a Harvard student in terms that could apply to millions of other naval-gazing undergraduates facing up to impending adulthood. Gates described himself 'sitting in my room being a philosophical depressed guy, trying to figure out what I was doing with my life'.

Doubtless, this is a broadly accurate depiction, in that the exact path of his life was yet to be laid out. However, whereas many students literally have not a clue about what will come after their carefree university days draw to a close, Gates was all but destined to make his mark in the computing industry. After all, he spent swathes of his waking hours honing his programming skills and had done for years. When Gates first got serious with a computer, he was only thirteen, but very quickly it was evident that it was a relationship built on firm foundations. He had found his love and was intent on nurturing it.

The 'first date' occurred around 1968 at Lakeside school, although it was something of a blind date. That is because Lakeside did not have a computer of its own. Such things were too large and much too expensive for a school to possess in those days. To own a mainframe computer – the cutting-edge machines of the time – you needed a budget of millions and acres of air-conditioned space in which the banks of equipment could be kept at a suitable temperature. Nonetheless, Lakeside did have a teletype machine, which could be connected to a mainframe housed elsewhere. Lakeside paid to use the mainframe on a time-share deal alongside numerous other institutions.

Although the computing that could be done within this system was rudimentary to say the least, the experience captured Gates's imagination instantly. He and a few other pupils set up the Lakeside Programmers' Club, and before long Gates had written his first chunk of original code – a program to run a game of tic-tac-toe. Never one to let his youth hold him back, Gates was the youngest member of the club but one of its most prominent characters. His refusal to cede time on the teletype machine eventually resulted in him being asked to leave the group, but he was soon back when the others realized he was capable of technical feats that they were not. He agreed to rejoin but, in typical Gates fashion, he insisted it would be on his terms. He returned as a more dominant figure in the club than the one they had exiled.

Nonetheless, there was still the thorny issue of economics. It cost students about $8 an hour to use the machine. That would be expensive for your average internet café today but in the late 1960s it was a small fortune for a schoolboy to find. For a while the group received funding from a parents' group, but it was not long before that revenue stream could not keep pace. Meanwhile, Bill's parents were stretching themselves to send him to the school in the first place and were in no position to bankroll his new hobby. So Gates did just what he has done all through his life – he used his initiative. He needed money, so he would find a job.

As chance would have it, the skills he had been developing would get him the position to pay for him to continue honing them. A company called Computer Center Corporation (or C-Cubed) had recently set up business in Seattle. Gates and his fellow Lakesiders struck an innovative deal with them. In return for finding bugs in the nascent company's programs, the students were granted access to C-Cubed's mainframe for free. Obviously, this had to be out of office hours, so Gates and his pals got into a culture of computing late into the night and at weekends. His work for C-Cubed would bring him to the attention of a company working on programs to analyse electricity needs in the Columbia Basin. Unaware that Gates was only in the ninth grade at the time, they called him in for an interview, which led to him taking up a valuable work placement in Portland. There he came into contact with a senior programmer called John Norton, who made an enduring impression on Gates, not least for the way in which he pushed the young boy to keep getting better. Gates hardly needed encouraging.

By the time he was fifteen, Gates had progressed far beyond games of tic-tac-toe. He joined forces with a club member a couple of years his senior called Paul Allen, beginning a professional relationship that would see both men reach the upper echelons of the world's rich list. But they started out humbly enough. Their first major venture was to write a program that took Seattle's raw traffic data and converted it into reports that could be used by traffic engineers. They called the program Traf-O-Data and ultimately made in the region of $20,000 from it. More importantly, they had gained invaluable experience and realized they worked well as a team.

While developing Traf-O-Data, Gates and Allen drafted in a third partner, Paul Gilbert, to work on creating hardware to run the program. It was an enterprise that convinced the two that in fact software was the way forward for them. A little while later, Gates created another program that automated the timetables of the teaching faculty at Lakeside. In return, he was given increased access to the mainframe that the school used. Gates was letting his expertise work for him and had the good sense to take the opportunity to develop further as his reward.

Gates may well have pondered what lay ahead of him in his Harvard dorm room. We know, for instance, that he flirted with the idea of following his father into law or perhaps becoming a scientist. But it is difficult to believe that there was really much doubt as to which road he would eventually follow.

THE BIRTH OF THE MICROCOMPUTER AGE

'Never trust a computer you can't throw out a window.'

STEVE WOZNIAK

In the late 1960s, modern computing was almost exclusively via mainframe computers – physically vast machines used by governments and businesses for mass data processing. Save for a few enthusiastic hobbyists cobbling together circuit boards in their spare rooms, the idea of individuals using a personal computer for their own ends was but a distant dream.

However, by the early 1970s, new vistas were opening up, thanks in large part to the rapid development of microprocessors. Around this time, Silicon Valley – as the Santa Clara Valley in California came to be known – was beginning to blossom as ever more high-tech companies (many with affiliations to Stanford University) gravitated to the area. Facilities such as the Xerox PARC research and development hub would exert a profound influence on the technological industry for decades to come, not least through the impact they made on Gates at Microsoft and Steve Jobs at Apple.

1975 would prove a truly landmark year in the development of the personal computer. That year a company called Micro Instrumentation and Telemetry Systems (or MITS for short) released the Altair 8800. Based on the Intel 8080 microprocessor released in 1972, it was a microcomputer that an adept hobbyist could build from kit. Furthermore, retailing at $439, it was just about affordable, too (although the price quickly rose as you added other bits of essential equipment).

In truth, the Altair 8800 does not much resemble the personal computers with which we are now familiar. It lacked a monitor and a keyboard and had a miserly 64K memory. This was not a machine on which you could stream movies or play *Grand Theft Auto*. Yet, it was to prove crucial in the PC revolution that was primed to spectacularly ignite. Not only was it the computer that directly led to the creation of Microsoft, but it also inspired another techy enthusiast, one Steve Wozniak, to build a machine of his own: the Apple I.

The world was about to change for ever.

Embrace Your Inner Geek

'If being a nerd means you're somebody who can enjoy exploring a computer for hours and hours late into the night, then the description fits me, and I don't think there's anything pejorative about it. But here's the real test: I've never used a pocket protector, so I can't really be a nerd, can I?'

BILL GATES, *THE NEW YORK TIMES*, 1996

There are photographs of Gates from his college days and the early years of Microsoft in which he looks nothing less than the poster boy for geekdom. Wearing shapeless jumpers over his small frame and sporting owl glasses and a dishevelled mop of hair, he could not have looked more like the class nerd if he had tried. If that were not enough, even his choice of childhood musical instrument was high on the 'uncool' scale. No guitar or saxophone for Gates, but the trombone instead.

Even when he had become one of the richest people on the planet, he showed neither enthusiasm nor aptitude for fashion. As he explained to *Playboy* in 1994:

> There was one point in my life when my mother was trying to explain to me about what colour shirt to wear with what ties … and I think people listen to their mother's advice when it relates to fashion.

It's not an area in which I claim to know more than she does … I don't look down at the colour I'm wearing during the day. So if it pleases other people that I know a little bit more about which shirt to pick with which tie, that's fine … I think I know a little bit about it now, but below average.

Yet if the youthful Gates seemed to epitomize 'the geek', the truth was always a little more nuanced than that. He may never have been the school jock, but he was an able athlete and, as we have seen, fiercely competitive. He *did* spend much of his life tapping away at computers, but his interests extended beyond, too. Yet, undeniably, there was still something about him that made entry into the 'cool gang' all but impossible.

His image was further enhanced by tales of his penchant for rocking back and forth, not least during meetings. As a child he had a rocking horse that he loved and upon which he spent valuable time contemplating the world. Though he outgrew the horse, the motion continued to soothe him into adulthood.

The boy Gates was also renowned for an extraordinary love of jumping. He enjoyed inserting himself inside a box and then springing out, trying to go further each time, and he continued polishing his jumping skills past the point when most of us would have left it behind as an infantile endeavour.

OFF THE SCALE?

There has been speculation over the years as to whether Gates exhibits traits consistent with autism. This is a claim without any known foundation, made more problematic by the fact that very many of us have aspects to our personalities that might put us somewhere on the 'autistic scale'. Nonetheless, in 1994 *Time* magazine ran a feature in which elements of his character and behaviour were compared with autistic traits. In particular, the article highlighted his highly logical approach to problems (needless to say, a computer programmer must have a certain love of order, although Gates was equally known for having an untidy desk), his ability for abstract thinking, his tendency (then, at least) to avoid eye contact and his reputation for sudden emotional outbursts. While such 'diagnosis at a distance' is intensely difficult and potentially dangerous, it nonetheless highlights Gates's enduring impression of 'otherness'.

Although he told the *New Yorker* in 1994: 'I don't jump spontaneously the way I used to, in the early years of the company … or even in a meeting …', despite going on to claim that his leaping exploits were now only rarely undertaken, it is known that he once took up a table-jumping challenge at a Microsoft Christmas party. Indeed, his future wife, Melinda French, was there, urging him on and ramping up the risk factor by placing lit candles on the tabletop.

The truth is, perhaps, that such endeavours reflect how easily bored Gates can become with ordinary life. For instance, Gates is left-handed (an attribute some research suggests is indicative of creative and innovative flair), and if as a student he found himself in a lecture that had lost his attention, he would take notes with his right hand for the simple challenge of it.

He has also historically seen himself as something of an outsider, even though he has rarely displayed a lack of confidence in social situations. In his early computing days, in which he was employed to find bugs in programs, he regarded himself less a coder than a hacker – that is to say, an outlaw-like figure. As he wrote in *The New York Times* in 1996: 'When I was a teenager, getting a computer to crash was a big deal. It was a way to learn.' Indeed, at one stage in his teens he was discovered hacking into a protected commercial program, and under threat of sanctions from both the authorities and his parents, he quit computing for several months.

By the time he was at Harvard, his sense of being

a social outcast had heightened. In a commencement address he gave at Harvard in 2007, he explained, 'I came to be the leader of the antisocial group. We clung to each other as a way of validating our rejection of all those social people.' Like many others before him, Gates had realized that if you can't join 'em, set up your own gang and be the master of that. If he wanted to sit at a computer, or jump out of a box, or rock backwards and forwards, then he would.

In recent times, his image has undergone something of a rehabilitation. For many years, he was caricatured as the corporate-lapdog uber-nerd against the curiously cool figure of Steve Jobs, who had carefully positioned himself as a champion of individuality and the 'think different' philosophy. But with his distancing himself from the day-to-day running of Microsoft, allied with his reinvention as the most important philanthropist of the age, the world has come to re-evaluate Gates. No longer is he simply the most famous tech guy on the planet, the leading light of what a famous 1996 documentary referred to as the *Triumph of the Nerds*. Instead he is seen as an intrepid fighter against disease, injustice and inequality. A sort of superhero, if you like. And there's nothing geeky about that. But Gates wouldn't mind even if there were. In 2011 he told the *Daily Mail*:

Embrace Your Inner Geek

Hey, if being a geek means you're willing to take a 400-page book on vaccines and where they work and where they don't and you go off and study that, you use that to challenge people to learn more, then absolutely, I'm a geek. I plead guilty. Gladly.

Keep an Eye on the Big Chance

'Let's start a company. Let's do it.'

Whatever uncertainty Gates felt about his future at Harvard, he seized his opportunities with vigour when they arose – just as he has continued to do throughout his life. Where a more cautious spirit might have held back and risk-assessed an opportunity, Gates demonstrated from a young age a sound instinct for making the right choices.

1975 was the year everything changed for Gates, in no small part down to Paul Allen and the Altair 8800. It was Allen who first saw an article in the magazine *Popular Mechanics* detailing the release of the groundbreaking new machine. He got in touch with Gates at Harvard and suggested the two work together to develop a language for it. The 8800 in its raw form was, to all intents and purposes, a box with some blinking lights, but Allen was convinced they could make it do so much more. As Gates told it years later, Allen implored him to join their fortunes together and form a company. They threw a few names around for the nascent enterprise. Allen & Gates (in that order) was one option, but they settled on Micro-soft (since they were anticipating creating software for microcomputers). The hyphen would be dropped within a few months.

There is a vast chasm between giving your theoretical business a name and breathing life into it. But Gates and Allen had the tenacity and audacity to make things work. They also had the fear – a fear that a software revolution was about to start and they might miss out on it. Now was their time to seize the moment and if they missed it, it might never return. Working on the principle of 'nothing ventured, nothing gained', Gates made an extraordinary approach to Ed Roberts, the founder of MITS.

He told Roberts that he and Allen (virtual unknowns, let it be remembered) had created an interpreter for the 8800 that would allow the machine to run programs written in BASIC – Beginner's All-purpose Symbolic Instruction Code, a computer language in popular use since the mid-1960s. Roberts was intrigued and arranged for a demonstration at the company's offices in Albuquerque, New Mexico, for six weeks later. Success! Except, of course, Gates and Allen did not yet have anything to show MITS. But cometh the hour, cometh the men.

The greatest problem they faced was that they did

not have access to an 8800, nor did they have the resources to purchase one. They did, however, have their acumen. Gates secured access to the mainframe computer at Harvard's Aiken Computer Center and he and Allen used the information available in the *Popular Mechanics* piece to create a simulation. They spent most of February and March working like dervishes, much of it in Gates's dorm room, and gradually created a suitable piece of software. Expending enormous energy, they strove to make it as neat, simple and elegant as possible. In their 1992 book *Hard Drive*, authors James Wallace and Jim Erickson quoted Gates thus: 'It was the coolest program I ever wrote.'

In the event, Allen was chosen to go to Albuquerque to demonstrate it, and continued to refine it even as he travelled to meet the MITS boss. Roberts was suitably impressed with what he saw (and entirely unaware of the circumstances of its rapid creation). He agreed to buy the package for $3,000 plus royalties. It would go on to become the industry-standard program for the next six years, fuelling Gates's determination that Microsoft should provide industry-standard software for evermore.

As a result of their success, Allen was recruited by MITS to be the company's software director. Gates took a brief sojourn from his Harvard studies to join him in Albuquerque, working as a contractor. Not long after his return to Massachusetts, he decided to make the move permanent. So it was that he dropped out of Harvard in June 1975. He and Allen decided to give Microsoft a real go in a bid to become leaders in an industry – the software business – that did not yet meaningfully exist. They could feel which way the wind was blowing, though. The age of the personal computer was looming and virtually no one (save for another hopeful start-up called Apple) was producing computers with their own software. That meant there were a lot of manufacturers in need of software to run on their machines. Steve Jobs neatly summed up the scenario in which Microsoft was born: 'Bill started a software company before anyone even knew what a software company was.'

The founding partners agreed that Gates should be president and Allen vice president. Furthermore, since Allen was receiving a salary from MITS, Gates persuaded him that he should have a 60 per cent stake and Allen 40 per cent. From the outset, Gates held to the notion that all is fair in love, war and business.

Buoyed by the MITS deal, Microsoft soon had a roster of other customers. Gates, meanwhile, was un-stinting in his efforts to drive the company on. Not only did he play his part in coding, but he looked after the administrative side of things and hit the road in search of new work. When the relationship with MITS came to an end in 1977, Microsoft no longer had a pressing reason to be in the relative technological backwater of Albuquerque. Gates and Allen were ready to go back home, so relocated the company to Bellevue, Seattle, in 1979. By then, they had thirteen employees. And within two years, the workforce had grown tenfold. By 1983 it had reached almost 500 (and would hover around 90,000 when Gates left his full-time post with the company in 2008). Gates had always prided himself on knowing every member of staff by name, but those days were soon over. Microsoft was in the big league and Gates could rest easy that the opportunity had assuredly been seized.

Find Your Comrades-in-Arms

'I'm not an educator, but I'm a learner. And one of the things I like best about my job is that I'm surrounded by other people who love to learn.'

BILL GATES, *THE ROAD AHEAD*, 1995

Gates possesses enormous personal resources and self-motivation, but he also realized early on that he needed to find like minds with whom to collaborate if he was going to fulfil his grandest dreams. Therefore, he has always maintained a small coterie of close confidants and allies whose skills complement his own. No matter how adept a coder, Gates understood that the software industry evolves so rapidly and in so many directions that a one-man band is doomed to fail. As the above quote suggests, a winning team needs members who are all prepared to learn from each other. Gates is blessed with sufficient self-belief that he is not afraid to work with people who may have skills that surpass his in certain areas, and who are unafraid to challenge him. As one of his most influential colleagues, Nathan Myhrvold, told *Time* in 1997: 'Bill is not threatened by smart people, only stupid ones.'

Over the following pages are profiles of a few of the most significant of Gates's brothers in arms – starting with Allen – who helped build Microsoft into the leading software firm in the world.

PROFILE: Paul Allen

Gates and Allen were school friends from Lakeside who worked together on the Traf-O-Data project and went on to co-found Microsoft. Before Bill and Melinda, people spoke of Bill and Paul. He was the Sundance Kid to Gates's Butch Cassidy, or, perhaps more pertinently, Woz to Gates's Steve Jobs.

Born on 21 January 1953, Allen is older than Gates but was always the quieter of the two, even at school. Their friendship was rooted in a shared belief that computers have the power to change the world. Early on in their association, Allen noted Gates was 'suggestible and ... ready to jump at any chance to have fun in strange ways. We fit together very well.'

The two maintained their relationship even after Allen left school to begin studying at Washington State University. However, Allen would never graduate, instead taking a job with a tech firm in Boston before joining MITS. Having co-founded Microsoft in 1975, Allen was there through the company's initial growth phase until 1983, when he left the business after being diagnosed with Hodgkin's disease. By then, Microsoft was unrivalled as the world's biggest software firm.

The Gates-Allen pivot worked so well because it was balanced. Both were hugely capable programmers, but while Gates focused on building the business in those early years, Allen ensured that the technological side was up to speed. Gates summed it up like this: 'I'm more aggressive and crazily competitive … running the business day to day while Paul keeps us out in front in research and development.'

If Allen was the perfect counterbalance to Gates, that is not to say that their friendship did not have its ups and downs. It is a fact they both freely admit. For instance, Allen quickly learned not to play chess against Gates, since the latter was a sore loser who typically swept the pieces off the board in a fit of pique when Allen had the effrontery to best him. Allen's 2012 biography, *Idea Man*, further elucidated their sometimes tempestuous relationship, with Gates noting that his memories differed to Allen's regarding certain events that depicted him in an unflattering light.

Notably, Allen suggested Gates had been keen to downgrade his partner's shareholding during the illness that ended his full-time role with the company. Even the very title of the book indicates that Allen feels he brought much to the partnership that has gone publicly unacknowledged. Yet for all the blow-ups and recriminations, they were undeniably a brilliant team. In 1997, Gates told *Time*: 'We were true partners. We'd talk for hours every day … we are very close friends today and I'm sure we always will be.'

> 'During the last fourteen years we have had numerous disagreements. However, I doubt any two partners have ever agreed on as much.'
>
> A LETTER GATES SENT ALLEN WHEN THE LATTER LEFT MICROSOFT IN 1983

Shortly after Microsoft went public in 1986, Allen became a billionaire and as of December 2014 had an estimated net worth of $17.1 billion. Yet, like Gates, he has hardly sat back and put his feet up. In 1986 he founded Vulcan Inc., which has come to embrace a number of varied enterprises. He is, for instance, the owner of the Seattle Seahawks American football team (who became Super Bowl champions under his leadership), the Portland Trail Blazers basketball team and the Seattle Sounders soccer team. Meanwhile, he has established the Allen Institutes for Brain Science and Artificial Intelligence, invested millions in a private space-exploration programme and was among the original backers of Steven Spielberg's DreamWorks Studios.

A great music lover (and sometimes rock guitarist in the band The Underthinkers), he has used his connections to secure jamming time with the likes of Paul McCartney, Mick Jagger and Bono. Having bought some extremely expensive pop memorabilia, including Jimi Hendrix's white Stratocaster, which he played at the legendary Woodstock Festival, Allen established the Experience Music Project (now the EMP Museum), a collection of popular cultural artefacts housed in a building designed by Frank Gehry. He has also built up a private art collection comprising works by the Old Masters that some experts consider among the most important on the American continent.

Then there are the yachts. Allen has owned at least three mega-yachts, including the 126-metre *Octopus* that cost $200 million in 2003, when it was thought to be the largest of its kind in the world. Employing a crew of between fifty and sixty, it includes a cinema, an industry-standard recording studio, a basketball court, a swimming pool and even its own eight-person submarine. Working with Gates may have had its challenges, but its rewards are evident too.

PROFILE: Steve Ballmer

Gates first encountered Ballmer at Harvard where they became firm friends. He joined Microsoft as its business manager in 1980 and headed up several divisions before becoming first the company president in 1998 and then succeeding Gates as CEO in 2000. It was a post he held until 2014, when his net worth was put at around $22 billion.

Ballmer, a native of Detroit, is a few months younger than Gates and was majoring in applied mathematics when they first met. Both were keen to further their business knowledge, so enrolled on a postgraduate economics course. Much of it went above their heads but it demonstrates the importance they attached to understanding the nuts and bolts of commerce. In addition, Ballmer managed the college football team, as well as writing for the *Harvard Crimson* newspaper and another literary magazine. Unlike Gates and Allen, Ballmer did graduate (magna cum laude, no less), but withdrew from further studies at the Stanford Graduate School of Business.

By 1980, Microsoft was growing so quickly that Gates felt the need for a business manager to assist him and could think of no better candidate than his former college friend. Ballmer was signed up as the company's twenty-fourth employee. Before long he had earned a reputation within the corridors of Microsoft as an enforcer and a voice-piece for Gates. If Gates could cow an employee with a tantrum, Ballmer was every bit as forceful. Although he lacked the technical savvy of the company's two founders, he was a passionate advocate for the business and would prove key to driving it to new commercial heights.

He would become head of several departments – including operations, operating systems development, and sales and support – and worked extensively in the US and European markets. When the time came for Gates to hand over the reins of power at the company he had birthed, Ballmer was his hand-picked replacement.

Ballmer is a risk-taker in the mould of all great entrepreneurs and puts much of Microsoft's success down to the management's willingness to make 'bold bets'. However, his championing of this tactic contributed to his tenure as CEO coming to an end. After a series of acquisitions had failed to reap their expected rewards, Ballmer found himself confronted by a board split over the proposed multi-billion dollar purchase of the Nokia mobile phone company. Although the sale went through, it was announced in August 2013 that Ballmer would step down from his role. It is also widely rumoured (although not confirmed) that Ballmer's relationship with Gates strained after he became CEO and that the two no longer talk. If it is indeed true, it is a shame, since before handing over the reins of power Gates had told *Forbes* that 'Steve is my best friend'.

Nonetheless, Ballmer proved that there is life after Microsoft, becoming owner of the Los Angeles Clippers basketball team a few months after relinquishing his post. He paid a princely $2 billion for the team. It should make for a tasty fixture against the Portland Trail Blazers!

PROFILES: Charles Simonyi, Nathan Myhrvold, Kazuhiko Nishi

If Allen and Ballmer were the most dominant figures at Microsoft alongside Gates, there are many others who contributed to the company's technological and commercial expansion. In fact, far more than can be detailed here. However, the three figures below all deserve special mention.

Hungarian-born **Charles Simonyi** is a software architect who was twenty when he moved to the United States in 1968. He worked for a while at the legendary Xerox Palo Alto Research Center (Xerox PARC), including a stint alongside the esteemed Robert Metcalfe developing an early personal computer, the Xerox Alto. In 1977 Simonyi earned a doctorate in computer science from Stanford Uni-versity and four years later he met Gates, who suggested he head up a new applications development division. In this post Simonyi oversaw the creation of Word, Excel and other

Office applications that provided the foundations for Microsoft's long-term fortunes. He left the company in 2002 to co-found his own business, Intentional Software. He also found himself in the public spotlight for his fifteen-year-long relationship with entrepreneur and celebrity, Martha Stewart. With a personal fortune estimated to be in eight figures, he has been able to indulge his love of space with two trips to the International Space Station. He has also undertaken substantial philanthropic activities.

Like Gates and Allen, **Nathan Myhrvold** is a son of Seattle. Born in 1959, he studied at UCLA and Princeton, where he completed a doctorate in theoretical and mathematical physics. He subsequently set up a tech firm that Microsoft bought in 1986 for $1.5 million. Myhrvold then began a thirteen-year stint with Microsoft, becoming its Chief Technology Officer and founding Microsoft Research in 1991. His fingerprints were on many of the innovations that drove Microsoft's rise to world domination in the 1980s and 1990s. His post–Microsoft life has included the establishment of Intellectual Ventures (a company specializing in patent management), winning the world barbecue championships and writing a book, *Modernist Cuisine*, about the application of scientific and technological approaches to food preparation. In 2010 his personal fortune was rated at $650 million.

Kazuhiko Nishi was born in 1956 in Kobe, Japan, and in 1977 he founded the ASCII Corporation, which published a popular computing magazine and became active in software development. Nishi – a somewhat plump engineering student – joined forces with Gates in 1978 when both were just twenty-two years old. Commonly known as Kay, Nishi became Microsoft's agent in the Far East and was responsible for securing a deal with the Japanese firm NEC that gave Gates his foothold in the region. He was also key in the discussions that led to Microsoft teaming up with IBM. As Gates would recall: 'That night Kay was the first guy to stand up and say, "Gotta do it! Gotta do it!" Kay's kind of a flamboyant guy, and when he believes in something, he believes in it very strongly. He stood up, made his case, and we just said, "Yeah!"'

But by 1986, the relationship between Kay and Gates had fallen apart, thanks largely to the former's unpredictability. This ranged from falling asleep in meetings (although Gates could hardly get on his high horse about that, as we shall see) to collaring high-level executives on their doorsteps and overriding financial instructions from Gates himself. With Microsoft about to float on the stock exchange, Gates wanted to restructure their partnership and bring Kay within the company on a full-time basis. But Kay would have none of it. The result was an acrimonious split. 'The guy's life is a mess,' Gates told the *Wall Street Journal* at the time. 'He's worth negative half a million and I'm worth X million – that's certainly seeds for bitterness.'

Employ
the Best

'We're very big on hiring smart people,
so you'd better be comfortable working
with other smart people …'

BILL GATES, 1998

Just as Gates has striven to fill his inner circle with people who share his vision and bring their own particular attributes to the party, he sought to build Microsoft on a bedrock of talented staff united in a common cause. As he said in a keynote speech at San Jose State University in 1998: 'We like people who have got enthusiasm for the product, technology, who really believe that it can do amazing things.'

Those who go to work for Microsoft (variously nicknamed Microsofties, Microserfs or the more generic Propellorheads) know that they are going to be put through their paces. Eighty-hour weeks, for instance, are not at all uncommon for many employees. Indeed, Gates was quoted by Daniel Ichbiah and Susan Knepper in their 1992 book *The Making of Microsoft* as saying, 'If you don't like to work hard and be intense and do your best, this is not the place to work.'

The demands put upon staff reflect Gates's enduring belief that Microsoft must always give good product.

'Microsoft is designed to write great software,' *Forbes* reported him as saying in 1997. 'We are not designed to be good at other things.' That, it would be fair to say, includes providing employment to slackers. But for those who make the grade, the rewards are plentiful. Not only is there the prospect of significant financial remuneration (although new employees shouldn't expect to get rich quick), there is also real scope to make your voice heard. In his 1999 book, *Business @ The Speed of Thought*, Gates stated: 'Smart people anywhere in the company should have the power to drive an initiative.'

In 2003, Gates gave an interview for the Smithsonian Institution Oral and Video Histories, which provided a unique insight into his attitude towards recruitment:

Our hiring was always focused on people right out of school. We had a few key hires like Charles Simonyi who came with experience. But most of our developers, we decided that we wanted them to come with clear minds, not polluted by some other approach, to learn the way that we liked to develop software, and to put the kind of energy into it that we thought was key.

In many ways, Gates always sought to replicate the formula that gave the company its initial successes:

a workforce full of uncynical, youthful exuberance, unstinting energy and a keen eye for the potential of the latest technology. Of course, that is bad news if your work starts to lag behind the curve. Although Microsoft has pretty impressive staff retention statistics by industry standards, it has long been rumoured that the 5 per cent of lowest-achieving programmers are culled each year. As Gates wrote in *The New York Times* in 1996 (in words imbued with a hint of menace): 'The flip side of rewarding performance is making sure that employees who don't contribute are carefully managed or reassigned.'

SLEEP IS FOR WIMPS

'We didn't even obey a 24-hour-clock; we'd come in and program for a couple of days straight.'

BILL GATES, *TRIUMPH OF THE NERDS*, 1996

Although life as a Microsoftie is not to be entered into lightly, it should also be noted that Gates did not expect more of his staff than he himself was prepared to do. He has always had a phenomenal – even macho – work ethic, routinely labouring until he quite literally dropped. The early days of Microsoft were littered with legendary marathon coding sessions, fuelled by copious amounts of pizza and punctuated by high-speed drives along New Mexico's highways. Continuing the quote above, Gates said, '[There were] four or five of us. It was us and our friends – those were fun days.' Senior staff were even known to doze off during client meetings, such was the effort they expended on product development. Meanwhile, at internal meetings, Gates liked to brainstorm while reclining on the floor, a habit that also commonly resulted in unscheduled naps.

To Gates, sleep is essentially for wimps. He wrote for *The New York Times* in 1997 that he envied those people who can survive on three or four hours' sleep a night, arguing they 'have so much more time to work, learn and play'. There is the nub of his attitude towards rest: while the medical profession assures us that sleep is essential for physical, mental and emotional well-being and development, Gates considers it something that happens while you could be doing something more constructive. Here was a man, after all, who reportedly took just fifteen days holiday between 1978 and 1984.

Nonetheless, Microsoft was also at the forefront of that movement in the 1980s and 1990s that looked to provide employees with workplace leisure opportunities. Rooted in the principle that a worker able to cut loose every now and again will return to their job energized, motivated and inspired, Gates created a headquarters at Redmond (not far from Seattle) famous for its atmosphere reminiscent of a university campus. There are, for instance, extensive on-site sports facilities, including football pitches, basketball courts and running tracks, along with catering services that stay open far later than your standard factory canteen. For many years the company also organized an annual summer Micro-Games (reminiscent of the mini-Olympics of Gates's childhood vacations at Hood Canal), before staff numbers made such an enterprise too unwieldy.

The Redmond Campus is unlike the offices most of us encounter in our professional lives. But just because you might see the staff dressed in civvies having just shot a few hoops, don't run away with the idea that this is a place where you can relax for too long!

Dare to Dream

'Our slogan from the very beginning was
"a computer on every desk and in every home".'

BILL GATES, 1997

In 2008, Gates told *PC Magazine* that 'I really had a lot of dreams when I was a kid'. His reluctance to ever put limitations on his imagination proved invaluable when it came to launching a business in a sector as unmapped as the software industry was in the 1970s. Gates never let fear of the unknown hold him back or constrain his ambition. It is perhaps telling that one of the early suggestions he and Allen considered for their company name was Unlimited Limited.

While it may have been Apple that coined the phrase 'Think different', it was a philosophy equally shared by Gates at Microsoft. 'Our business strategy from the beginning was quite different than all the computer companies that existed when we started,' Gates told an audience at San Jose State University in 1998. 'We decided to focus just on doing the high-volume software, not to build hardware systems, not to do chips, just to do software …' Strange as it might sound in this age of myriad software developers, such a move took enormous courage, but Gates did not flinch for a moment.

While pragmatic and occasionally ruthless in his business dealings, he did not get into the game simply to make fast bucks. Like most truly great entrepreneurs, he has always worked to a long-term strategy. In his 2008 *PC Magazine* interview, he continued, 'We [Microsoft] have a longer time horizon than anyone else.' Furthermore, although a natural businessman, he regards himself as a scientist and innovator first. In 1994, for instance, he said in an interview with *Playboy* magazine, 'I devote maybe 10 per cent to business thinking. Business isn't that complicated. I wouldn't want to put it on my business card. I'm a scientist.' Two years later, he was quoted in Randall E. Stross's *The Microsoft Way* as saying, '… the future is what matters, which is why I don't look back too often.'

It was his mix of determination and vision (allied with Allen's, too) that saw Microsoft establish a foothold in the emerging industry during the late 1970s and early 1980s. The pair quickly built a team of nine core employees and by 1980 the company had a staff of thirty-two. Deals with the likes of MITS, Commodore and Apple ensured there was plenty of work for busy hands. Then Gates made the deal of his life (see page 57) with the then undisputed giants of the computer industry, IBM. At the time, IBM had a workforce in excess of 300,000, giving a ratio of approximately 10,000 staff to each one at Microsoft. It was a commercial engagement of David-and-Goliath proportions, yet Gates had the foresight to demand terms that would see Microsoft eventually outstrip IBM in terms of market value many times over.

In 1983, *Time* magazine broke with its custom of anointing a 'Person of the Year' by instead choosing the computer as 'Machine of the Year'. Gates and Jobs were the individuals most identified with the revolution then in full swing. A year later Gates featured on a *Time* cover for the first time in his own right. Two years after that, Microsoft went public, propelling Gates towards becoming the youngest billionaire in the world. It was an extraordinary rise, from naval-gazing college dropout to global icon in just over a decade. Yet it was not, perhaps, anything beyond what Gates had hoped for himself back in 1975, when he and Allen discussed their dreams for the future, epitomized in the quotation at the beginning of this section: 'a computer on every desk and in every home'. What had appeared mere sci-fi to some was rapidly turned into reality by Microsoft.

And still Gates aspired to more. The introduction of the graphical Windows operating system in 1985 (imperfect as it was in its early guises) alongside the Office suite of software applications (including Word for word processing and Excel for spreadsheets) saw the company go from strength to strength. By the mid-1990s it had secured utter world domination (a term used advisedly) of the software market and then, albeit a little belatedly, rode the internet wave. Such success allowed for yet more dreaming. 'We can afford to make a few mistakes now, and we can't afford not to try,' he was quoted as saying by Brent Schlender in *Fortune* in 1995. '… Everything's about big horizons at Microsoft now. But, hey, we can tackle big horizons. We're expected to tackle big horizons. We *love* big horizons.' A taste of his vision of the future was reported in the same publication by Randall Stross two years later: 'The future of computing is the computer that talks, listens, sees and learns.'

In more recent years, Gates has brought the same level of vision to his philanthropic activities and to addressing the biggest challenges our planet faces. Consider his take on fighting climate change by developing renewable energy sources, as reported by *Wired* in 2011: 'If you're going for cuteness, the stuff in the home is the place to go. It's really kind of cool to have solar panels on your roof. But if you're really interested in the energy problem, it's [massive solar plants] in the desert.' The words of a man who never dreams small.

MICROSOFT'S BIG DEAL

'I was the mover. I was the guy who said, "Let's call the real world and try to sell something to it."'

BILL GATES, QUOTED BY JAMES WALLACE
IN *HARD DRIVE*, 1992

In 1980, Gates struck the deal that elevated Microsoft from an emerging player in the software industry to a global super-company. From annual turnover of around $2.5 million, it would soon be doing business in terms of billions.

The opportunity came when the world's most recognizable name in computers at the time, IBM, decided to dip its toe into the personal computer market. There is no doubting that IBM was quite brilliant in its traditional areas of expertise: providing technological hardware for businesses and large organizations. But this was something entirely different. By the 1980s the company was such a giant that it struggled to be quick and agile – two characteristics that the youthful Microsoft had in spades.

It was an open secret in Silicon Valley that IBM was struggling to create a satisfactory operating system for its personal computer. Gates and the Microsoft team had inevitably come on to their radar and the IBM management decided to approach them as they sought an out-of-house solution. Gates might still have been only in his mid-twenties, but they recognized him as an emerging master in their sector, blessed with an old commercial head on young shoulders.

It is said that when Gates first met with the suited-and-booted IBM team, he turned up in a rather dishevelled state, sporting trademark slacks and a cotton-knit shirt. Everyone felt suitably awkward so that the next time they met, Gates broke with tradition to wear a shirt and tie while his counterparts opted to dress down Gates style! Regardless of their disconnect when it came to clothing, Gates did his best to offer them useful advice. In the first instance he suggested IBM approach one of Microsoft's regular commercial partners, Digital Research Inc., since Microsoft did not have an operating system of its own to offer them.

Sadly for Digital Research, but not for Gates and his team, negotiations fell through, so the IBM execs returned to plead for help from Gates. He agreed to develop an operating system on their behalf. Just as with the MITS deal a few years earlier, Gates had promised something not yet in his possession, so adopted a suitably pragmatic approach as he sought to keep up his side of the bargain.

He contacted a Seattle programmer by the name of Tim Patterson, who had recently created an innovative operating system called Q-DOS (Quick and Dirty

Operating System). Gates paid him a one-off fee for rights to the product. Though estimates differ on the exact amount, it is thought to have been in the region of $50,000, which was surely among the best money Gates ever spent (especially given that it now barely even counts as small change in his world). Microsoft then set to work on reconfiguring Q-DOS for IBM's needs, and unveiled it as MS-DOS (Microsoft-Disk Operating System). Relieved, IBM signed it up and marketed it as PC-DOS.

Gates knew the pressure IBM was under and if he had been of different character might have attempted to extract the greatest possible immediate financial benefit from them. Instead he took a quite different approach, anchored in his belief that the real rewards would come by engineering the deal to establish a dominant share of the operating systems market. Therefore, he struck a bargain in which IBM got MS-DOS for a relatively low, one-time up-front fee. Crucially, though, Microsoft retained copyright of the product. Gates was taking a punt, but he wagered that lots of companies would begin manufacturing machines on the IBM model and when they did, he would have a ready-made operating system solution to sell them. It was a calculated risk, and it paid off handsomely.

The IBM PC retailed with a choice of three software

packages, of which PC-DOS was one. By letting IBM have it at little expense, it was also the cheapest of the options. This was critical to Gates's long-term plan, since he knew ultimate success relied on first becoming the IBM PC package of choice. Sure enough, its low price point helped PC-DOS assume top spot among consumers. Given its clout in the computing field, IBM inevitably shifted a lot of units and sales escalated, with Microsoft's name spreading as the go-to software people. PC-DOS became the industry standard. Furthermore, just as Gates hoped, other manufacturers (over 100 of them) soon came knocking to licence MS-DOS. Meanwhile, other major hardware manufacturers including Sony, NEC and Matsushita asked Microsoft to provide them with their own bespoke systems. In monetary terms, the company's sales more than doubled between 1980 and 1981. Before long, Microsoft was far and away the leading name in the booming global software business.

Innovate,
Innovate, Innovate

'We tell people that if no one laughs at at
least one of their ideas, they're probably
not being creative enough.'

BILL GATES, *THE NEW YORK TIMES*, 1996

In 2003, Bill Gates told *Newsweek*:

> A breakthrough is something that changes the
> behaviour of hundreds of millions of people where,
> if you took it away from them, they'd say, 'You
> can't take that away from me.' Breakthroughs are
> critical for us. All we get paid for are breakthroughs,
> because people who have our software today can
> keep using it forever and not pay us another dime.

It is this determination to keep pushing the technological boundaries and to be first to deliver products
that consumers want that has ensured Microsoft has
been at the top of the pile for coming on four decades.
But while Gates understands as well as anyone the
financial incentive to innovate, he also sees a bigger
picture. As he told *MIT Technology Review* in 2010,
'Believe me, when somebody's in their entrepreneurial
mode – being fanatical, inventing new things – the

value they're adding to the world is phenomenal.' Whatever one may think of Microsoft as a company, no one can deny that its products have changed the way the world works (and plays).

For a long time, Gates's reputation as a hard-nosed businessman rather belied his status as a considered thinker, but those who have kept a close eye on him have never underestimated his strengths in that direction. Rich Karlgaard, the publisher of *Forbes*, once said, 'The old distinction between ideas and products, between ephemera and ingots, is evaporating.' Gates in many ways personifies this change.

His love for innovation in computer technology is genuinely profound. When in 1996 the *Smithsonian* magazine asked which moment he would choose to revisit in history, he opted for the invention of the transistor at the Bell Labs in 1947. It was, he said, 'a key transitional event in the advent of the information age'. He is also a man who genuinely fears being overtaken by the opposition. In his 1994 book, *Showstopper!*, G. Pascal Zachary quoted Gates thus: 'You always have to be thinking about who is coming to get you.' (Such a feeling is widely shared in the dog-eat-dog world of Silicon Valley, as suggested by Andrew Grove, chairman of Intel and a man Gates much admires, who chose to call his autobiography *Only the Paranoid Survive*.)

Gates knows that failure is only a misstep or two

away and that there is no shortage of pretenders to the throne. 'In a fast-moving industry,' he said in a speech in California in 1997, 'the companies that are successful are those that are able to get out in front of the key trends and really add value in the new applications.' In the same year, he told *Businessweek*, 'At Microsoft, we take the long-term view. That means we invest a lot in research and development to help us understand future directions, while staying competitive in terms of product development today.' Nathan Myhrvold, Microsoft's then Chief Technology Officer, put it even more bluntly: 'The only way to get access to strategic technology is to do it yourself.'

DON'T REST ON YOUR LAURELS

Gates used the cautionary tale of the fabled Xerox PARC to spur him to press onward in developing new products. Established by a company that made its name in printing, Xerox PARC pioneered a series of technological breakthroughs in the 1970s, not least in personal computers, but failed to make commercial capital out of them and lost out to the likes of Apple and Microsoft. Gates was determined not to follow the same ill-fated path.

Therefore, Gates spent much time and effort creating an atmosphere conducive to research and development. In his interview for the Smithsonian Institution Oral and Video Histories in 2003, he said:

> Every three years are important in terms of redefining what we do. Any company that stays the same will be passed by very quickly and there are lots of fine examples of that ... I was always thinking that the environment [where] we did product development should be a fun environment, a lot like a college campus.

Indeed, Microsoft garnered a reputation for its student-like atmosphere and a certain level of acceptable goofing amid all the product development.

He is on record as describing software as a blend of artistry and engineering, a mixture that requires time to ferment. As he told *Advertising Age* in 1996, 'People must have time to think about things.' And in a speech he gave at St John's College, Cambridge, in 1997, he said, 'Part of the beauty of research is getting the greatest minds together without any deadline.' Certainly, updated versions of Windows are notorious for their delayed releases, sometimes by as much as a couple of years. But Gates has fiercely defended his company's right to hold back a product until it is market-ready. 'If you take quality as a given,' he told *InfoWorld* in 1994, 'you are always going to have some uncertainty in the date … the date is not the fixed thing for any of these products. Period. It's not.'

He has also traditionally favoured creating small teams to develop ideas, telling the *Financial Times* in 1996, 'Size works against excellence. Even if we are a big company, we cannot think like a big company or we are dead.' The ideal is a team no bigger than thirty-five people to work on any given project, a model he attempted to adhere to even as the company's expansion went into overdrive. If Microsoft was one big team, he craved mini-organizations all functioning within the larger body. 'Small teams can communicate effectively and aren't encumbered by a big structure slowing them down,' he was reported as saying in *Industry Week* in 1995. In addition, he has promoted an approach to research and development that puts the customers' needs and desires at its heart and which seeks elegantly simple solutions. 'The barrier to change is not too little caring; it is too much complexity,' he said in his commencement address at Harvard in 2007.

Certainly, the Microsoft Labs have largely avoided the disappointments that afflicted Xerox PARC, a place where ideas were fostered, bloomed and then exploited by other companies. Boasting a roster of products as era-defining as MS-DOS, Windows,

Office, Internet Explorer and the Xbox, Microsoft has an admirable track record in staying ahead of the curve and capitalizing on it achievements. As quoted by George Taninecz in the same *Industry Week* interview in 1995, Gates reflected, 'The entrepreneurial mindset continues to thrive at Microsoft because one of our major goals is to reinvent ourselves – we have to make sure that we are the ones replacing our product instead of someone else.'

STRESS-TEST YOUR IDEAS

'Conflict is at the heart of every significant Microsoft decision. This is a company constantly at war, not only with outsiders, but also with itself.'

G. PASCAL ZACHARY IN *SHOWSTOPPER!*, 1994

Given that ideas are at the heart of his business and his world view, Gates treats them pretty seriously. When a good one appears to come along, he likes to test it out, stretching it to breaking point. Only those that spring back into shape are accepted. He is a man who says that a good manager should never have to revisit a decision, because they will have done their homework and know it was the right call first time round (see page 79). So once an idea has gained his acceptance, you can be sure Gates believes in it and will fight for it.

Nonetheless, getting to that stage can be an arduous process. Stories are legion of Gates taking apart a suggestion put forward by some hopeful colleague, with little energy expended on saving the other person's feelings. He is known to shout and rant in meetings, effortlessly dishing out caustic put-downs and never afraid to engage in a confrontation – all in the interests of testing a hypothesis, of course. He is nothing short of Darwinian in his approach, believing that only the strongest ideas deserve to and will survive.

He is known in particular for his refrain that an idea is 'the dumbest [insert optional expletive here] thing I ever heard' – a line destined to undermine even the hardiest and most self-confident of souls. But Gates genuinely believes that this is a valid way of proofing an idea, rather than an affront to the individual who proposed it in the first place. As he told *Playboy* in 1994:

I've never criticized a person. I have criticized ideas. If I think something's a waste of time or inappropriate I don't wait to point it out. I say it right away. It's real time. So you might hear me say 'That's the dumbest idea I have ever heard' many times during a meeting.

Many have fallen victim to a Gates tongue-lashing, and a few have never really recovered, but he is a man who respects being challenged, too. While there are those who have accused him of a bullying demeanour, by the same token he respects those who stand up to him and defend their corner. In a 1990 staff video, a Microsoft programmer by the name of Chris Peters advised: 'Never hide anything from Bill because he's so good at knowing everything. But you should be firm, and you should yell back … But say no. Bill respects no.'

Gates is also willing to admit that sometimes he gets it wrong. Nathan Myhrvold – who regularly took part in high-level brainstorms with him – was always impressed by his boss's ability to admit as much. That, though, is all part of the Gates method by which he hopes only the very best ideas will make it through. If it is a strategy that is not always pretty, it has been undeniably effective.

Gates and Intellectual Property

'Our great successes come with an approach of embracing anything that's popular and then coming along with extensions … to embrace everything that's out there and make it easy for systems to co-exist.'

BILL GATES, 1997

The ideas business (especially one as fluid and rapidly evolving as the software trade) raises many thorny questions concerning the laws of intellectual property (IP). It is one area in which it is possible to detect inconsistency in Gates's approach, largely depending on whose intellectual property is in question.

According to the World Intellectual Property Organization, IP refers to 'the creations of the mind, such as inventions; literary and artistic works; designs; and symbols, names and images used in commerce'. To the wider world, it is all that stuff legally protected through patents, copyright and trademarks, often denoted with little symbols on merchandise. But establishing exactly what constitutes intellectual property is a tricky business, and one with huge financial implications. As a result, Bill Gates and the Microsoft legal team have hardly been strangers in the law courts of America and beyond over the years. They have been involved in numerous cases where they stood accused of misappropriating intellectual property, just as they have accused others of doing the same.

On the one hand, Gates's early career involved him legitimately developing and extending other people's creations. The deal with MITS, for instance, saw him create a product that exploited the extant BASIC language, and he then modified an existing operating system for IBM – in both cases, quite legally. He has always been adamant that Microsoft has never stolen but instead is happy to embrace that which already exists and work to make it better.

Few serious technology historians dispute the fact that Silicon Valley was born out of a fairly liberal sharing of ideas, a melting pot in which ideas evolved. In such a climate, inevitably there are those who feel they missed out on their deserved credit for innovating something entirely new. The victor was often the one who could finesse an idea and get it to market first. As Gates noted in an internal Microsoft memo in 1991: 'If people had understood how patents would be granted when most of today's ideas were invented, and had taken out patents, the industry would be at a complete standstill today.' In other words, if developers had been wilier about patenting from the start, there would never have been the exchange of ideas that allowed the industry to evolve as quickly as it did.

Gates and Intellectual Property

Yet there is another side to Gates that is fiercely protective of IP. When just starting out in the business, he wrote an impassioned letter that appeared in a popular hobbyists' magazine, criticizing those amateur enthusiasts who illegally copied Microsoft software. His argument was simple: that developers had the right to be paid for their work. In his words at the time: 'As the majority of hobbyists must be aware, most of you steal your software. Hardware must be paid for, but software is something to share. Who cares if the people who worked on it get paid?' If they were indeed denied that right, a key imperative to serious development would disappear. In short, everyone would lose out.

Certainly, Microsoft has come to fiercely embrace the world of patents, pursuing those it believes to be in violation of the law. In 2004, Steve Ballmer alleged that the Linux operating system breached some 235 Microsoft patents alone. Patents have thus become a big part of the Microsoft business, generating billions in revenue each year and keeping a whole division occupied. Meanwhile, the company argues that proper management of patents is essential to fostering technological breakthroughs.

Gates has adopted a similar approach in his philanthropic activities, arguing that IP law has a crucial role to play in the development and distribution of innovative

PATENT LIKE GATES

Remarkably, Microsoft received its first patent only in 1986 and by 1990 had less than ten to its name. However, the internal memo sent round in 1991 seems to have marked a sea change in approach. Fearful that 'some large company will patent some obvious thing related to interface, object orientation, algorithm, application extension or other crucial technique' and thus reap years of resultant profit, Gates's solution was 'patent exchanges with large companies and patenting as much as we can'. By 2009, Microsoft had notched up its ten-thousandth patent, and files somewhere in the region of 2,500 new applications each year.

solutions to the world's biggest problems. Why, for instance, should a drug company spend big on developing a cure for a disease rampant in sub-Saharan Africa if it cannot expect a sensible return on its investment?

Such an approach does not always play well with his critics, particularly given that it is reported he once commented: 'Intellectual property has the shelf life of a banana.' Furthermore, there are plenty of people willing to accuse Gates of being less concerned with IP that does not belong to him.

For instance, in 1997 the *Wall Street Journal* quoted Daniel Bricklin, senior technology developer with Trellix Corp, about working with Microsoft: 'It's very scary to be dancing with an elephant. They look at what you're doing and borrow whatever they can.'

Doubtless the most famous IP case that Gates has fought (and won) pitted him against Steve Jobs and Apple. After Microsoft released Windows, Apple sued the company, alleging Gates's team had stolen the 'look and feel' of Apple's graphical user interface made popular by the success of the Mac. The case dragged on for several years before the courts found for Microsoft in 1994 and raised many interesting questions as to what constitutes intellectual property, as well as what counts as theft and what is legitimate development of existing technology. Gates was particularly candid on the subject, giving a nod to the debt that both companies owed to the research work done at Xerox PARC. In a now legendary exchange at Apple's offices described by Walter Isaacson in his 2011 biography of Jobs, the Apple boss yelled at Gates, 'You're ripping us off! I trusted you and now you're stealing from us!' Gates coolly fired back, 'Well, Steve, I think there's more than one way of looking at it. I think we both had this rich neighbour named Xerox and I broke into his house to steal the TV set and found out that you had already stolen it.'

Lead from the Front

'I wouldn't call "sensitive" a birth attribute of Microsoft, or even of Microsoft's senior management.'

STEVE BALLMER, REPORTED IN THE *WALL STREET JOURNAL*, 1998

Looking like the eternal schoolboy and with a vocal tone and delivery not especially suited to rousing oratory, Gates is not the prototype of the great leader. With a penchant for using slang exclamations such as 'Supercool!', he is unlikely to ever be mistaken for a Winston Churchill. Yet, in many ways he has evolved into one of the most significant leaders of the modern age. He has shown in two disparate fields (software and philanthropy) that he combines creative thinking, pragmatism, organization and the ability to inspire those around him.

As has already been noted, Gates garnered a reputation for frequent abrasiveness when dealing with staff and colleagues at Microsoft. As well as the casual insults, interruptions and coruscating sarcasm, he would break out into bouts of apparently uncontrolled shouting and screaming (although one suspects that he knew just what he was doing). Then there was his disconcerting habit of rocking while deep in thought and his tendency to simply stare down questions he did not want to answer. Many of his employees grew to fear the summons to meet their boss. He himself would tell *Newsweek* in 2000, shortly after he had stepped down as CEO, 'It was an inhuman job. It makes infinite demands on you.'

Yet being a good company boss has never been about being the most popular guy in the office. Despite being sometimes difficult to deal with (a fact attested to by the occasionally strained relations he had even with senior figures like Allen and Ballmer), he has commanded great loyalty and delivered undeniable results. Contrary to initial appearances, he possesses a plethora of leadership attributes that come naturally to him. As he revealed to the Smithsonian Institution Oral and Video Histories project in 2003, his desire to lead from the front was there even in his school days. Referring to the occasion when the Lakeside Programmers had thrown him out and then invited him to return, he explained, 'In high school I told the other programmers, "Look, if you want me to come back you have to let me be in charge. But this is a dangerous thing, because if you put me in charge this time, I'm going to want to be in charge forever after."'

Although the desire to lead is indicative of a certain egotism, Gates also understands that a truly great leader nurtures an organization that can prosper almost independently of its chief. At the 2006 press conference in which he announced he was relinquishing his full-time post with Microsoft, he said, 'The world has had a tendency to focus a disproportionate amount of attention on me.' Leadership for Gates is thus less about self-aggrandizement than about being in a position to see things are done to his exacting standards.

He has an enviable ability to keep focused on the task at hand and has never been shy to put in the time and effort to guarantee his businesses operate as he wants. Aside from his willingness to work long hours, he approaches his job in a highly methodical way. For instance, he rarely attends a meeting without being fully briefed on all the issues to be covered. In 1996 he commented in *The New York Times*, 'When I go to a meeting, I keep specific objectives in mind. There isn't much small talk, especially if I'm with colleagues I know well.' It is his firm belief that a bit of legwork early on saves unnecessary labour later. Once he has stripped away the niceties to get to the heart of a matter, he is confident in his ability to make the right call at the first time of asking.

'Don't make the same decision twice. Spend time and thought to make a solid decision the first time so that you don't revisit the issue unnecessarily.'

BILL GATES, 1997

He also runs tight ships in which decisions are predicated on a combination of evidence and instinct. Every member of staff is expected to be able to justify why and how they do what they do, while new ideas are put under microscopic scrutiny. Yet, he also allows himself the freedom to trust his gut. As he told *Time* in 1997, 'I don't think that IQ is as fungible as I used to. To succeed, you also have to know how to make choices and how to think more broadly.' It was a subject he revisited in his widely reported 2008 speech on creative capitalism: 'Rationality only goes so far.'

If all of this sounds like Gates takes his leadership roles very seriously, it should also be remembered that he puts a high value on fun, both for himself and those with whom he works. His sporadic lapses into bouts of juvenile goofing around once prompted Ed Roberts (the MITS chief) to observe: 'He's kind of like Elvis Presley; he never got to grow up.' It is true that he possesses a certain Peter Pan-ish quality, and not just in appearance. He retains a wide-eyed belief that anything is possible and a youthful faith that he is the person to make it so. In a speech at Columbia University delivered in 2009, he said:

There become a few magic moments where you have to have confidence in yourself. You have a few moments like that where trusting yourself and saying yes, this can come together – you have to seize on those because not many come along.

Furthermore, you get the real sense that he will not give time to labours that don't fire his enthusiasm. Take his comment to *Time* in January 1997 about his work: 'I still feel this is superfun.' But perhaps he said it best in a piece for *The New York Times* a year earlier:

Even today, what interests me isn't making money per se. If I had to choose between my job and having great wealth, I'd choose the job. It's a much bigger thrill to lead a team of thousands of talented, bright people than it is to have a big bank account.

His contribution as CEO was summed up in 1998 by Alan Brew, a branding consultant quoted in the *Wall Street Journal*: 'Bill Gates is Microsoft ... The character of the whole company is cloned in the form of this combative, young, arrogant leader.'

Learn from Your Mistakes

'Your most unhappy customers are
your greatest source of learning.'

BILL GATES, *BUSINESS @ THE SPEED
OF THOUGHT*, 1999

It is notable that many of the world's greatest sportsmen report that the satisfaction they get from their greatest victories is relatively short-lived. Their desire to go on to scale new heights depends less on recapturing the joy of triumph than on avoiding failure. This is a trait that Gates shares. Revelling in success is not for him. Instead, his face is always turned towards the next challenge. As he put it in 1995's *The Road Ahead*: 'Success is a lousy teacher. It seduces smart people into thinking they can't lose.'

It was a topic he had discussed a year earlier in an interview with *Playboy*. Then he had observed, 'Fear should guide you, but it should be latent. I have some latent fear. I consider failure on a regular basis.' It is the ever-present concern that one is about to be found out that has driven him to cast an ultra-critical eye over achievements that most mere mortals would take as evidence of sublime excellence. In his 1999 investigation into modern entrepreneurship, *Masters of*

Enterprise, H. W. Brands quoted Gates thus: 'I've always been hard core about looking at what we did wrong. We're not known for reflecting back on the things that went well. We can be pretty brutal about the parts that don't do well.'

Despite creating the world's leading software firm and becoming the richest man in the world, Gates still has a few mistakes to mull over. In the early stages of Microsoft's growth, his single biggest regret was allowing a Utah-based software business, Novell, to steal a march in the then emerging field of local area networks (LANs). LANs are networks into which several computers may be hooked up within a defined geographical area. In replacing the previously dominant mainframe computer model, they were vital in birthing the PC age. And Gates hated missing that particular boat.

Another notable failure was Microsoft Bob, an animated character the company released in the late 1990s to provide user help. Unfortunately, it was a piece of software that required such high-spec hardware on which to run that it often proved more a hindrance than a help and failed to win many fans. On that occasion, Gates concluded that the company had overdelivered beyond what the market was ready for. (For the record, it is to be hoped he did not go to town berating the project's manager, who just happened to be one Melinda French – the future Mrs Gates.)

But for Bill Gates, every failure is ultimately an opportunity to be better next time. As he put it in 1998:

There is a tendency in companies to let good news travel fast. Oh, we just won this account. Oh, things went so well. But the thing about good news is, it's generally not actionable … Bad news, on the other hand, is actionable … The sooner you get the bad news, the better off you're going to be, in order to kind of absorb it, to change your product plan, to go back and talk to the people, really dig into it.

THE INTERNET: THE ONE THAT NEARLY GOT AWAY

'Sometimes we do get taken by surprise. For example, when the internet came along, we had it as a fifth or sixth priority …'

BILL GATES, 1998

By the early 2000s, Microsoft's Internet Explorer web browser had secured virtual market dominance. Although new arrivals such as Firefox and Google Chrome have claimed some ground, it remains arguably the best-known browser of them all. Yet things might have turned out very differently, because for a short while in the mid-1990s, the World Wide Web looked like it might be the great big party that Microsoft was late for. It serves as a story that on the one hand illustrates how complacency can strike anybody, and on the other epitomizes Gates's knack of coming good when it really matters.

THE ORIGINS OF THE INTERNET

The internet as we know it today really has its origins in the 1960s, and in particular in the US Department of Defense's Advanced Research Projects Agency's ARPANET network, which was used to connect staff at various research facilities. It was not, however, a system intended for mass use. At a time when the dream of a fully functioning personal computer was still unrealized, the idea of plugging the general populace into a global information highway was little more than science fiction.

Even as the likes of Microsoft helped bring to fruition its vision of a computer on every desk, development of interconnected networks outside of seriously large (and rich) organizations lagged behind. However, in 1989 a seismic shift occurred when Tim Berners-Lee, a British computer scientist and once an employee at CERN (the European Organization for Nuclear Research), delivered a proposal for a system of linked 'hypertext' documents that could be viewed using a browser. Within two years the World Wide Web was alive and kicking, and the internet revolution was upon us.

At this time, Microsoft was still transitioning from a company with a firm focus on providing practical computing solutions for the business world to one geared up to serve private individuals. That may partly explain why it was caught off guard by the sudden rise of the internet as a plaything for billions around the world, as opposed to simply a tool for large institutions. Whatever the reason, the Microsoft developers did not have their eye on this particular ball until, in 1995, Gates realized it was an oversight that might kill them.

In May that year, he sent staff a memo entitled 'The Internet Tidal Wave'. In it, he described the internet as 'the most important single development to come along since the IBM PC was introduced in 1981'. Microsoft simply could not afford to ignore it. 'The Internet is a tidal wave,' he went on. 'It changes the rules. It is an incredible opportunity as well as incredible challenge.' He did a good job of hiding his panic. A couple of years later he would admit that things had reached 'fever pitch' in the company, but took solace that the crisis was, albeit belatedly, acknowledged – evidence, he said, that Microsoft's nervous system was alive and well.

With Gates pushing his developers as hard as ever, within a few months the company announced the arrival of its own browser, Internet Explorer (IE). By bundling it with Windows, IE became the most widely used browser on the planet, eclipsing the hitherto giants of the arena such as Netscape. To some, Microsoft looked like nothing less than a schoolyard bully, using its corporate muscle to elbow its rivals out of the way. Such was the robustness of its approach that the Department of Justice launched its anti-trust investigation. But in the end, Microsoft emerged un-scathed bar a few hefty fines, which its revenues comfortably covered. Where it had looked for a while like the internet phenomenon would explode without them, Gates realized his oversight just in time and was able to thrust his business to the forefront of the revolution.

Gates's words in a speech he gave in Washington in 1997 are instructive. Describing the internet boom, he said, 'The closest thing to it I can think of is the Gold Rush where everybody went off to find their fortune. And people were fairly surprised at how it all turned out.'

Keep Track of the Competition

'Whether it's Google or Apple or
free software, we've got some fantastic
competitors and it keeps us on our toes.'

BILL GATES, 2010

There is no doubt that the ultra-competitive streak of Gates's personality helped drive the success of Microsoft. Whether competing in a race in the mini-Olympics of his childhood, playing a game of chess against a young Paul Allen or facing off against Steve Jobs over the development of graphical user interfaces, Gates has only ever been content to emerge the winner. And like any great fighter, he strives to make sure his own game is up to scratch while looking for weaknesses in his opponent.

Not that Gates has ever been foolish enough to think that he can (or indeed needs to) vanquish every rival in sight. He has also had the good sense to seek out natural allies along the way. He approached MITS at a time when they offered him just the foot up the ladder that he needed, and when it came to really hitting the big time, he tied his colours to the mast of the acknowledged industry leaders of the day, IBM. He even joined forces with Apple when it suited his purposes, going so far as to help them out in several hours of need. As he wrote in *The Road Ahead* in 1995: 'Our success has really been based on partnerships from the very beginning.'

Gates grasped from the outset that rather than attempting to clear the playing field of all competition, he would be better served simply by keeping a close and critical eye on it. That way he could fathom when an alliance would bring benefits and, even more importantly, when his rivals were stealing a potential march. It is then that the demon wannabe chess master has emerged, as Gates's brain whirrs to figure out how to shut down the opposition's advantage and regain the upper hand himself. As he told CNN in 2008: 'All good capitalistic companies get up every morning and think, "How can we make a better product? What are they doing well? We're going to make it cheaper, better, simpler, faster."'

In addition, such is his critical eye that he believes that he cannot only replicate the strengths of his rivals, but can spot potential advantages that they themselves are yet to realize they have. As he wrote in his column for *The New York Times* in 1996:

We focus on what other companies do well as opposed to what they do poorly. We don't dismiss a company as unimportant just because a lot of things about it may be less than perfect. The company may be doing something important; it may not even know that it is important.

Gates has also consistently backed his vision over those of his commercial rivals. Where some people get nervous if their ideas seem *too* different to everybody else's, Gates revels in them. For him, there is rarely the self-doubt that wonders if an idea unshared is somehow intrinsically flawed. Like the greatest inventors and entrepreneurs, it is the search for the brainwave that has eluded everyone else that drives him on. Speaking in 1995, he put Microsoft's success down to nothing less: 'We had ideas that the giants of the time missed.'

This last comment, though, is indicative of one blind spot when it comes to competition: Gates – like Jobs and countless other self-made successes – struggles to recognize that he and the company he created gained 'giant' status themselves long ago. As such, behaviour that might have appeared feisty and courageous when he was a 'David' setting out on his career path can look like the actions of a bully when executed by a 'Goliath'. As he explained in 1995, 'The outside perception and inside perception of Microsoft are so different. The view of Microsoft inside Microsoft is always kind of an underdog thing.'

Although expressing a view that rather clashed with the reality of Microsoft's already well-established dominance, it opens a window on to how Gates has seen himself for much of his adult life: as the plucky little guy taking on the big boys and doing whatever is needed to succeed.

MICROSOFT vs. APPLE

> 'They [Microsoft] just have no taste. I don't mean that in a small way. I mean that in a big way, in the sense that they don't think of original ideas and they don't bring much culture into their products.'
>
> STEVE JOBS, 1996

Of all the commercial rivalries in Bill Gates's career, none has been as utterly diverting as that which existed with Steve Jobs. Indeed, it is fair to say that it is one of the most intriguing match-ups not only of the technological revolution of the last forty years, but in all the history of commerce. In its own way, it has been epoch-defining.

In key respects, the two were very similar. Both good American boys from relatively comfortable backgrounds who showed early precocious talent, they each dropped out of college to follow their dreams of making it big in the same emerging business sector. In addition, both liked to be in charge, commanding reputations for spikiness and ruthlessness, while demanding the highest standards from those who worked with them. And both, of course, built their businesses into global powerhouses, earning unimaginable personal fortunes in the process.

Perhaps it was the fact that they could sense so much of themselves in the other (along with their mutual competitiveness) that made their personal relationship so fiery. Jobs hardly helped matters by carefully manipulating his image so that for a long time he set himself up as an appealing 'outsider' figure against Gates's establishment geek. Yet, for all that they clashed, the two had a certain chemistry and evolved a friendship that was genuine, if grudging. It is often said that one should keep your friends close and your enemies closer. In this case, though, that does not seem sufficient to explain quite what drew the two to each other. Doubtless, they came to have real respect for what the other had achieved.

Admittedly, there were some basic philosophical differences too, although these should not be overstated. While Jobs always promoted his machines as tools for private individuals intent on 'thinking different', Gates initially focused on the needs of business. And where Jobs had an eye for aesthetics, Gates's strengths lay more with functionality. Yet, whatever their differences

'I'd give a lot to have Steve's taste.'

BILL GATES ON STEVE JOBS, 2007

in approach, they had an instinctive understanding that the presence of one made the other even stronger. They might have been going after some of the same market, but if either one of their companies did not exist, that market itself would have been exponentially smaller. The computer business was plenty big enough to accommodate them both.

Of the two, Jobs was by far the more antagonistic, at least in public – as the quote at the start of this section indicates. If there was an opportunity to attack Microsoft as a company and Gates as an individual, he found it difficult to resist. On another occasion, for instance, he told an interviewer that Gates would have been a 'broader' guy 'if he had dropped acid once or gone off to an ashram when he was younger'; it really was playground stuff.

It is perhaps all the more surprising, then, that the two businesses worked as closely together as they did. Furthermore, to an independent eye it looked very much like Apple needed Microsoft more than the other way around. Take as an example the deal Jobs struck in 1982 whereby Microsoft agreed to create a spreadsheet, database and graphics program for the

Mac. Gates could not have been more magnanimous, declaring in a speech in 1984:

> To create a new standard, it takes something that's not just a little bit different; [but] something that's really new and really captures people's imagination. And the Macintosh – of all the machines I've seen – is the only one that meets that standard.

As Microsoft surged ahead of Apple in terms of commercial success, the relationship between the two great figureheads deteriorated. It must have been a particularly difficult situation for Jobs to handle, since he also knew that Apple would face a real struggle without Microsoft software such as Word and Excel, whereas Microsoft could take comfort in the notion that were Apple to disappear overnight, another computer manufacturer would take its place and no doubt want to run Microsoft products too.

Jobs's strategy was, characteristically, to go on the attack. The tactic was best epitomized by his decision to sue his counterpart on charges of ripping off the Mac's graphical user interface in the production of Windows. That the case was all but thrown out of court hardly warmed relations, and both Apple and Microsoft kept plenty of lawyers in clover for many years as they arm-wrestled over patents and copyright.

Keep Track of the Competition

By the time Jobs returned to Apple in 1997 for a second term as boss, having been unceremoniously dumped twelve years earlier, both he and Gates had mellowed. That, it might be suggested, is what age and a few billion bucks in the bank can do for you. At the time, Apple was but a shadow of the cutting-edge company it had been during Jobs's first tenure, with much of the industry convinced that its best days were behind it. With his astute grasp of commercial reality, Jobs found the humility to strike another bargain with his old nemesis.

Microsoft bought some $150 million of Apple stock and agreed to keep producing software for its computers. Not only did this give Apple a fighting chance of re-establishing itself as a major player, but Microsoft's investment was deemed a very public show of confidence by the biggest name in the global computing business. Jobs, as ever, had no intention of understating its importance: 'I think the world's a better place for it.' Nonetheless, when a giant image of Gates was beamed into 1997's Macworld convention (the company's giant annual trade show), Apple fanatics began an impromptu round of booing. It was evidence of the poison that Jobs had spread against his rival over the years, and at that moment a rather embarrassing example of biting the hand that feeds.

As Gates's retort to Jobs about their burgling of Xerox PARC showed, the Microsoft maestro was no pushover in private and it may be assumed he gave as good as he got in the face of Jobs's sporadic antagonism. Yet he continued to make public utterances that cast his opposite number in a good light. For instance, in his speech at San Jose University in 1998, he graciously noted:

In terms of an inspirational leader, Steve Jobs is really the best I've ever met. I mean, he can make people work, you know, more than they should. He's got to be careful, it's such a strong power, he can overuse it. He's a first-class magician, I'm kind of a second-class magician.

In 2007, the two even shared a public stage amid a notably chummy atmosphere at the *Wall Street Journal's* D: All Things Digital conference. At once complimentary and mindful of their contrasting approaches, Gates said, 'The way he goes about things is just different, and I think it's magical.' And when Jobs was nearing the end of his life – he died in 2011 after a long battle with cancer, aged just fifty-six – Gates visited him at his home, where they spent hours chatting informally across a broad range of subjects and reminiscing about their roller-coaster careers. To have been a fly on the wall to listen to their conversation would no doubt have been fascinating.

'Steve and I first met nearly thirty years ago, and have been colleagues, competitors and friends over the course of more than half our lives. The world rarely sees someone who has had the profound impact Steve has had, the effects of which will be felt for many generations to come.'

BILL GATES AFTER STEVE JOBS'S DEATH

Certainly theirs was a rivalry that inspired them to new heights – something for which anyone who has ever used a personal computer should be grateful. Despite its sometimes acrimonious tone, theirs was also a battle that in the end left no losers. Each played their own vast role in the technological revolution that has redefined the world since the 1970s. To steal a phrase from Jobs, they each made a formidable 'dent in the universe'. Perhaps the greatest curiosity is that their legacies may not be quite as the world once expected. While Microsoft appeared to have won the commercial battle in the mid-1990s, Apple overtook Microsoft as the world's most valuable tech company by market capitalization in 2010 – thanks to Jobs's masterful roster of twenty-first-century products, including the iPod, iPhone and iPad. Meanwhile, where Jobs once carved out a niche as the people's champion, Gates's emergence as the world's greatest philanthropist may yet win him the personal popularity contest. Gates, we might say, was the broad one after all – acid or no acid.

Business is Business

'Business is a good game: lots of competition and a minimum of rules. You keep score with money.'

BILL GATES, 1996

Whatever good Gates achieves with his super-sized personal fortune – and he has already done great things – it is fair to say that in its accumulation he was happy to play hardball. As Philippe Kahn, one of the founders of the software firm Borland, once observed: 'Gates is one hell of a sharp businessman.'

Gates might have regarded himself as principally a computer scientist, but he was also one of the great CEOs of the age. That he could for so long combine his talents as a product developer with the day-to-day demands of balancing the books and managing thousands of staff is a quite phenomenal feat. But he embraced the dual role of technologist and businessman from the moment he and Allen set up business together. 'I think the success of Microsoft,' he explained in 1993, 'has come from knowing these things have a relationship with each other. The two sides drive each other.' But, as Warren Buffett once said, 'If Bill had started a hot-dog stand, he would have become the hot-dog king of the world.'

Certainly, Gates has always strived to keep his approach to business uncomplicated, once saying, 'I think business is very simple. Profit. Loss. Take the sale, subtract the costs, you get this big positive number. The math is quite straightforward.' It seems those postgraduate lectures he attended with Steve Ballmer at Harvard were clearly not a waste of time! And if the proof of the pudding is in the eating, it is difficult to fault his approach. As of late 2014, Microsoft was the world's second most valuable company (behind, you guessed it, Apple) with a market capitalization of $410 billion and a global workforce approaching 130,000.

Yet the company's real economic heyday was under Gates's reign as CEO. From a two-man operation scrambling to write code for MITS in 1975 in return for a few thousand dollars, Gates grew Microsoft into the biggest company in the world, a title it took in 1997 when it reached a valuation of $261 billion. For anyone who had the ready cash and good sense to invest $2,100 in 100 shares when Microsoft went public in 1986, their holding would have earned them $1.4 million in late 1999, when the Microsoft stock price reached new heights. On 30 December that year the company recorded the hitherto highest market capitalization value in history of $618.9 billion – a record eclipsed by Apple on 20 August 2012 when it ended the day's trading with a market capitalization of $623.5 billion.

But Gates never let himself get carried away by such brain-scrambling numbers. Ever wary of growing complacent on success, he was never less than sanguine about the company's prospects. 'Microsoft won't be immortal,' he wrote in *The New York Times* in 1997. 'All companies fail. It's just a question of when.' Presumably keen to avoid sending the markets into a spin, he ended on a slightly more positive note: 'My goal is to keep my company vital as long as possible, of course.'

KEEP AN EYE ON THE BOTTOM LINE

As CEO, Gates ensured he never went on overly irresponsible spending splurges at the company's expense. Although eventually treating himself to that ultimate billionaire's plaything – a private jet – he has nonetheless always maintained a close eye on the bottom line. For instance, in a move that no doubt won the approval of Buffett, he had a habit of booking himself into economy class when flying, even though he could probably afford to buy the airline of his choice on any given day. As he argued in 1995, 'Flying economy costs less money. You get there just as fast as flying first class. And my body fits. If I was really wide or really tall, I might view the issue differently.'

Furthermore, Gates is ruthless in the boardroom. His determination to get the best deal possible, even if one has to step over a few bodies to secure it, is hard-wired. For proof, consider an episode from his early childhood when he approached his older sister, Kristi, with a business proposition. She was the proud owner of something Bill yearned for – a baseball mitt. Unable to afford the cost of a new one of his own, he instead offered her a princely $5 in return for unlimited and exclusive access to the said sports equipment. He even wrote up the terms in a contract that he got her to sign.

He mined such experiences when he began real deal-making as an adult. An expert, as we have seen, in squeezing every possible advantage out of a commercial hook-up, he also became highly skilled at protecting his interests when things went wrong. And with each potential setback that he overcame, he learned and became battle-hardened ahead of the next challenge.

While Microsoft owed its initial success to the MITS deal Gates and Allen so brilliantly secured, the subsequent collapse of the professional relationship between the two organizations brought Gates face-to-face with harsh commercial realities. The problem stemmed from a clause in the initial contract that required MITS to make 'best efforts' to promote the BASIC interpreter that Microsoft had produced for them. Gates and Allen received a royalty on each one sold, supplementing the fairly paltry initial payment they had received for the product. However, such was the level of piracy, Gates felt MITS had lost the appetite to actively promote it. So he set about reclaiming his copyright.

By then, MITS had been bought by a company called Pertec, who withheld payments while arbitration was ongoing. As Gates told it to *Fortune* in 1996, Pertec was 'trying to starve us to death'. He came close to settling, but in the end chose to see the fight through. The arbitrator, unimpressed by the conduct of both Pertec and MITS, found in Microsoft's favour. Not only did Gates win back the rights to sell licences to other companies, he also reached the conclusion that with the MITS partnership dead, Microsoft had no reason to remain in New Mexico. Making the best of what had been a tough situation, he and Allen agreed to return home to Washington state.

In a career as long and dramatic as Gates's, there have inevitably been other deals that misfired. Aside from the sometimes rocky road Microsoft trod with Apple, the next great falling out was with IBM. Things came to a head in the late 1980s during the development phase of OS/2, the successor to MS-DOS. 'It's easy for people to forget how pervasive IBM's influence over this industry was,' Gates recalled in *Triumph of the Nerds* in 1996. 'The relationship between IBM and Microsoft was always a culture clash. IBMers were buttoned-up organization men.'

In part, the problem seems to have been that the IBM programmers came to feel they were doing more than their fair share of the work. Gates, on the other hand, argued that if the Microsofties were creating less code, that was indicative not of laziness but greater efficiency. Compounding the dispute was a fundamentally different view on what an operating system should be. Gates wanted to create an open platform that could be utilized by many different hardware and software designers. This fitted with the ethos quoted in Paul Carroll's 1994 book, *Big Blues: Unmaking of IBM*. Gates is quoted discussing Microsoft's 'low-cost, high-volume approach in which any company, including our competitors, can write software and create hardware that works with the open Windows platform'. He contrasted this with IBM's 'high-cost, low-volume, proprietary approach'. Given their irreconcilable differences, it was perhaps little surprise when IBM effectively divorced Microsoft in 1992. Despite being battered by the experience, Gates again showed his robustness, leading his firm onwards and upwards. As history shows, it was not OS/2 that conquered the world – an object lesson in showing an ex that you can flourish without them.

Gates is an entrepreneur who has absorbed his fair share of hard knocks on the way to the top. But he never turned away from a fight, bouncing back from each knock-down stronger than before. His fighting spirit is summed up by a comment he made in 1994 when asked if the US government's anti-trust investigation might curb his competitive instinct: 'For me to become gun-shy might require surgery.'

MICROSOFT AND MONOPOLIES

'As you know, a monopolist, by definition, is a company that has the ability to restrict entry by new firms and unilaterally control price. Microsoft can do neither.'

BILL GATES, 1998

When Microsoft began in 1975, it consisted of two unknowns who dreamed of conquering the world, but such was their success that Microsoft was only the spunky underdog for a short while. Within a few years, the firm became the big bruiser able to throw its weight around. Suddenly it was other companies who could claim underdog status, and they were not slow to complain about how Microsoft conducted itself. As such, Microsoft has fallen foul of anti-trust laws (designed to prevent monopolies and to promote fair competition in the marketplace) in territories around the world, incurring fines of billions of dollars in the process. Yet Gates has always been adamant that Microsoft's success came about because it was better than the opposition, not because it stifled them.

The company's record of anti-trust disputes is unenviable. It was, for instance, the recipient of the single biggest fine ever given to a company by the European Union for violations of anti-trust legislation. In 2004, the European Commission imposed a fine of some $666 million in response to Microsoft's bundling of Windows Media Player into its operating system. In addition, it was compelled to share aspects of its coding. After the Commission deemed Microsoft 'non-compliant' with the judgement, it handed down a second fine of $1.4 billion in 2008. A further $731 million fine followed in 2013 for the company's failure to promote internet browsers other than IE to its European customers.

But it was an anti-trust action brought by the US federal government in 1998 that is the most notorious in Microsoft's history, not least because for a while it threatened the very future of the company. It was the way that Microsoft had bundled Internet Explorer into the Windows operating system that was the bone of contention. Because so many computers ran on

Windows, it was argued that bundling the browser into it effectively forced a purchase and unfairly restricted the chances of competitors, including original web trailblazers such as Netscape.

After several rounds of hearings, a judge decreed that Microsoft should be split into two separate entities – one devoted to its PC operating systems and another covering its other interests, including the Office suite and IE. However, that ruling was subsequently overturned on appeal and Microsoft eventually reached a settlement with the US Department of Justice that allowed it to continue as a single entity.

It was undoubtedly the greatest ordeal of Gates's career, but characteristically he fought his corner with vehemence. It also illuminates Gates's attitude towards the free market and Microsoft's place within it. His comment to *Playboy* in 1994 – just as the nightmare of the Department of Justice investigation began unfolding – encapsulated his position: 'The hard-core truth is that we've done nothing wrong.' To all intents and purposes, he has always rejected all claims of monopolistic tendencies on the basis of lack of opportunity and intention.

For instance, in 1998 he asserted, 'The beauty of the internet is its openness. It cannot be controlled or dominated or cut off.' Meanwhile, the *Wall Street Journal* quoted him as saying, 'It is not, nor has it ever been, the intention of my company to turn the information superhighway into a toll road.' Gates clearly felt aggrieved, believing that his company was coming under unfair scrutiny simply because it was successful.

His logic was straightforward: Microsoft had started out as a tiny company, but by bringing to market the products consumers wanted, it had come to dominate its competitors. This, as far as he was concerned, was not monopoly in action but the triumph of the free market. As he put it to *Time* in 1997: 'Who grew this market? We did. Who survived companies like IBM, ten times our size, taking us on?' He concluded that the US government's case was only that Microsoft's products were 'too capable' and he treated dismissively the suggestion that Microsoft ought to sell products with certain features absent in the interests of promoting competition in the market. Such products, he said, were nothing less than crippled, which was not what the free market was meant to be about.

Although cogently argued, his defence nonetheless failed to satisfy many of his critics, who consistently pointed out the reality that Microsoft's dominance was such that competitors struggled to get a foothold in the marketplace. Again, we come back to the David and Goliath analogy. Microsoft started out a David – small, agile, reliant on wits rather than muscle. In Gates's mind, his firm never changed. David simply carried on using the same tactics to vanquish all comers. But to much of the world at large, David had usurped Goliath and had himself then grown until he was simply Goliath 2.0. Heavily armoured, with a vast arsenal of weapons at his disposal and a fearsome reputation, Goliath 2.0 had become unassailable. There was simply no place on the battlefield for others.

While Gates, with some justification, insisted that neither he nor his company could be blamed for the fact that people bought their software in such volume, he could not fail to recognize the practical impact of Microsoft's might. He is simply too intelligent for that. For proof, one need look no further than the record of the proceedings of the Rosen Research Personal Computer Forum for May 1981. At a point in history when Microsoft was about to surge into the commercial big league thanks to its tie-up with IBM, Gates noted:

I really shouldn't say this, but in some ways it leads, in an individual product category, to a natural monopoly: where somebody properly documents, trains, promotes a particular package and through momentum, user loyalty, reputation, sales force and prices builds a very strong position with that product.

In certain respects, Microsoft's case was not helped by the reputation it had gained for aggressively making acquisitions. The company had branched out from its pure software beginnings to encompass interests in the hardware and wider media sectors. This was natural enough, given, for instance, Gates's enduring fear that the hardware industry would fail to keep progress with the software becoming available. What better way to drive that side of the computing business than by wielding a financial interest? In a speech he gave in 1998, he outlined other reasons for Microsoft to buy up companies:

A lot of the time, the reason we do the acquisition is, when we see a market developing very rapidly … we want to reduce the amount of time it takes us to get in there [to] get working with customers, [to] get the feedback that's valuable.

Although a compromise was reached with the Department of Justice that seemed to keep everybody's pride satisfied, the episode left Gates genuinely bruised. Of course, in fulfilling his dream of being king of the computer world, he had at times been ruthless in his treatment of rivals and rarely shirked a marketplace confrontation. But the line between legitimately pursuing market share and unfairly impeding rivals is thin and often up for grabs.

Gates's disappointment at the turn of events was palpable. He spoke of a witch-hunt and accused rivals of hiring lobbyists to stir up this particular hornets' nest. The Justice Department, on the other hand, would come to accuse Microsoft of adopting a legal strategy that was 'an affront to the court's authority'. Gates's personal discomfort comes through in this observation from 1998: 'When your own government sues you, it's not a pleasant experience. I wasn't sitting there going, "Ha ha ha, I'll do what I want." I was thinking, this is the worst thing that's ever happened to me.'

If the US anti-trust case was the nadir for Microsoft in terms of charges of monopolism, it was by no means the end of such litigation. As well as the case brought by the European Commission, the company also came under investigation in a number of other territories, including Japan and South Korea, while in 2014 there were reports that the Chinese government was about to start looking into Microsoft's practices. Still, the question remains: How big is too big? It is a conundrum with which Gates and his legal advisors have long wrestled.

Realize That No Man is an Island

'Amazingly, Melinda made me feel like getting married. Now that is unusual! It's against all my past rational thinking on the topic.'

BILL GATES, *PLAYBOY*, 1994

It is a Hollywood staple that in high school it is the jocks who get the girls, while the geeks get the grades ... until some glamorous and admirably deep cheerleader-type sees that, in fact, her future lies with a nerd and not the numbskull quarterback she was previously dating. While this depiction does not quite summarize Bill Gates's romantic history (and severely understates his wife's own significant accomplishments – she is more Michelle to his Barack Obama than Vanessa Hudgens to his Zac Efron) – it nonetheless hints at an underlying truth.

As it has already been noted, Gates is not and never has been an Adonis; he had a look that was never going to set hearts fluttering in the style of a Brad Pitt or George Clooney. Furthermore, he spent an awfully large part of his formative years busying himself at computers, which is hardly the most conducive way of building personal relationships (especially in an era before social networking). But this is not to say that

Gates had no luck with the ladies as a young man. Not everybody, after all, wants an Adonis, and Bill's undeniable boyishness held its charms for some. He was competently athletic too, quirkily smart and well rounded, and never lacked self-confidence. As he started making waves in the technology world, the press pictured him with a number of dates on his arm.

Perhaps most famously, he dated Ann Winblad – a leading Silicon Valley venture capitalist – on and off for three years or so after meeting in 1984. However, Gates could never quite shrug off the impression that dating kept him away from the really important business of software development. With little prospect of marriage, the pair split amicably and have reportedly remained on good terms ever since. As Gates put it in 1993: 'It certainly took me a lot of time, being a single person.'

It was not that Gates could never see himself settling down, but merely that he was yet to be at the point where it fitted into his life plan. Let's not forget, when he dated Winblad, he had not even earned his first billion! So it was always going to take someone special to turn him round to the idea of sharing his life on a permanent basis. And he met her – in the guise of Melinda French – in 1987. Perhaps against expectation, he was happily married before his fortieth birthday.

Although he hardly took his foot off the professional

accelerator, it marked a true turning point in his life. The arrival of children (Jennifer Katharine in 1996, Rory John in 1999 and Phoebe Adele in 2002) sealed the deal. Speaking to *Wired* in 2010, he said, 'When you choose to get married and have kids, if you're going to do it well, you are going to give up some of the fanaticism.'

All the evidence suggests he is as accomplished a family man as he was a CEO. At the time of writing, he and Melinda are into their third decade of marriage and Gates took to parenting with an ease that surprised some observers. The key, it seems, is that he found it fun from the outset.

In a 1998 *20/20* television interview, he said, 'My priority in life is my family. I always knew I'd get married and have children. You know, family life is all about being emotional and sharing things and doing things with each other.'

He has even drawn parallels between parenthood and the couple's philanthropic work. The *New Yorker* quoted him in 2005 on the subject:

We have taken on the top twenty killers and for everything we do we look at the cost per life saved and real outcomes in terms of how things get improved. It's fun, and it is also an enormous responsibility ... That is true for being a parent.

Many of the most important things in life are like that. Why else would you want to get up in the morning?

The overlap between these two spheres of his life has a financial dimension, too. He has been adamant that his children should have as 'normal' an upbringing as possible – quite an ambition when you are as rich, famous and powerful as Bill Gates. To this end, he is determined that their identities should not be defined by his wealth. His intention of pouring the majority of his wealth into his and Melinda's foundation has the knock-on effect of restricting what he can pass on to his offspring. In 2011, the *Daily Mail* reported him as saying, 'It will be a minuscule portion of my wealth. It will mean they have to find their own way. They will be given an unbelievable education and that will all be paid for.'

Of course, a minuscule portion of a gargantuan amount is still, to use a not entirely technical term, quite a lot. The Gates children will doubtless inherit riches that the rest of us can only begin to imagine. However, while they will likely lack for nothing, they will not simply be handed riches that most nation states – let alone private individuals – would envy. As he put it to CNN in 2008:

I don't think it would be beneficial to them to have huge amounts of wealth. I think that's very distortive in terms of how you think of the impact you're going to have, how you measure yourself, how your friends think about you and how they do things with you. And it's also bad for society.

There was a time when Gates was wedded to his career and it seemed quite possible that his devotion to growing Microsoft might be a bar to nurturing personal relationships. In the event, Gates's adult life has operated in three distinct fields: Microsoft, philanthropy and family. He has managed to input enormous energy and resources into each – evidence of a remarkably well-rounded personality. It was the great metaphysical poet John Donne who wrote that 'No man is an island.' Gates goes to prove the sentiment holds even if that man has the cash to buy an island or two of his own.

PROFILE: Melinda Gates

'Could you go out two weeks
from this coming Saturday?'

MELINDA GATES, RECALLING BILL FIRST
ASKING HER OUT ON A DATE, 2013

Being the wife of a man like Bill Gates may bring obvious advantages, but it is a hard task, too. By broad consensus, Melinda Gates has executed the role with aplomb, exhibiting intelligence, style and dignity. While Bill is inevitably the 'headline act', she has been more than a supportive wife and doting mother to his children in the background. An accomplished executive in her own right, she came into her own within the context of the Gates Foundation. There she has emerged as a key influence in its decision-making processes, a steady guiding hand and a notably skilled advocate for its causes. While never 'fluffy', she gives the foundation's image a welcome air of tender compassion, rather as Princess Diana achieved in her charitable works. As Gates has admitted, 'Melinda bonds with some constituencies more naturally than I do.'

But just who is the woman who claimed the heart of one of the planet's most powerful men? Melinda Ann French was born on 15 August 1964 in Dallas, Texas. Her family are staunch Roman Catholics and she attended a Catholic girls' school, the Ursuline Academy of Dallas. (Its Latin motto, '*Serviam*', translates as 'I will serve' – a fitting credo for the pupil who would go on to make such a splash in philanthropy.) Like Bill, Melinda showed an early aptitude for mathematics and was regarded as a diligent and accomplished pupil.

In a further parallel with her future husband, she was also sporty and competitive, proving herself a doughty long-distance runner and also excelling as a kayaker. Outdoor activities remain a passion for the couple, with their Lake Washington home an ideal base from which to pursue them.

From school (where she graduated as valedictorian in 1982) she progressed to Duke University in North Carolina, studying computer science and economics. Her star again shone brightly, with some of her professors circulating her papers among her fellow students. Singled out for great things, she was set on a fast-track that saw her receive first her bachelor's degree and then an MBA in a mere five years. Given Bill Gates's pride in Microsoft's ability to spot graduate talent, it was no surprise when the company recruited her straight from university (despite the fact that the French family had owned Macs and Melinda had previously been an intern at IBM!).

Moving to Seattle, she was among the brightest of the graduate intake, getting posted across the country to work as a project manager. As well as her technical prowess, she won recognition for her people-management skills (something Bill might perhaps have learned from) and her ability to coax a team into working to its potential. Even with the odd hiccup in her résumé (such as the ill-fated Microsoft

Bob initiative), she was soon established as a 'Very Good Thing'.

It was about four months after joining Microsoft that Melinda French found herself sat next to her husband-to-be during a dinner at a New York trade fair. He was, she later recalled, 'funnier than I expected him to be'. He, meanwhile, was instantly impressed by her independent spirit, her intelligence and her sense of humour. However, it was several months before the boss got round to asking his executive out. The setting was unglamorous – a car park – and Gates's suggestion of a date two weeks hence failed to sweep her off her feet. She suggested the proposition lacked spontaneity and he should call nearer the time. Having pondered her words, he called her later the same evening and suggested they meet that night. If she expected to be wined and dined, she was disappointed. He was talking at a computer users' meeting so the date ended up taking place at his house in the small hours. It did, though, give them an opportunity to really talk and get to know each other. He had also proved he could be spontaneous.

Communication has underpinned the enduring success of their relationship, within the dual contexts of their marriage and the foundation. In his 2010 book, *Working Together: Why Great Partnerships Succeed*, Michael D. Eisner quoted Gates as saying that they 'enjoy sharing ideas and talking about what we are learning'. They also make a habit of reading many of the same books as each other and setting aside time to converse about them as a way of keeping the spark alive. 'You've got to put energy into making sure you know what the other person's thinking,' Gates has gone on record as saying.

In 1993 he finally decided to pop the question, buying an engagement ring from a company owned by his old mate Warren Buffett. Buffett rather mischievously told Gates that he had spent fully 6 per cent of his net worth when buying an engagement ring for his wife-to-be in 1951, and suggested Bill should do likewise. Given Gates's wealth at the time, that would have equated to over $500 million. Whatever the final cost, we can rest assured that he spent more than the going rate, and the happy couple proceeded to celebrate their betrothal by throwing a lavish *Great Gatsby*-themed party, with Gates as Gatsby and Melinda as Daisy Buchanan.

They married on New Year's Day in 1994 on a beach on the Hawaiian island of Lanai. Shortly afterwards, Melinda – who is fiercely protective of her privacy – left Microsoft, where she had risen to be general manager of its information products division. In 1996, the first of the Gates children arrived, but she continued to hold several directorships, including a seat on the board of the *Washington Post*, and was a trustee of her old university.

In 2005, *Time* gave their 'Persons of the Year' title to 'The Good Samaritans', symbolized by the Gateses and Bono – 'three people on a global mission to end poverty, disease – and indifference'. As the accolade cemented Melinda's emergence as a major public figure in her own right, her importance to the running of the foundation was confirmed by Bono himself: 'Lots of people like Bill – and I include myself – are enraged and we sweep ourselves into a fury at the wanton loss of lives. We need a much slower pulse to help us to be rational. Melinda is that pulse.'

Just like her husband, Melinda built her career on sound academic foundations (indeed, she is famously more highly qualified than her 'drop-out' spouse) and a passion for technology. But it is as a mother and a philanthropist that she has found her greatest satisfaction. Consider her words to an audience at Stanford University in 2014:

Optimism for me isn't a passive expectation that things will get better; it's a conviction that we can make things better – that whatever suffering we see, no matter how bad it is, we can help people if we don't lose hope and we don't look away.

Enjoy the Trappings of Your Success

'Ridiculous sums of money can be confusing.'

BILL GATES, *PLAYBOY*, 1994

The rise of the techno-billionaires at the end of the twentieth century recalled the emergence of America's industrial millionaires in the nineteenth century. As media magnate David Geffen noted to *Forbes* in 1994: 'It is still possible to be a Vanderbilt, an Astor, a Rockefeller.You can still do that; you can be Bill Gates.' For the last thirty years and more, America has been comparatively awash with uber-rich self-made men (for they mostly are men) with ready cash burning holes in their pockets. Philanthropic endeavours aside, how has Gates chosen to spend his wealth?

Much of it is tied up in his myriad ongoing business interests, which extend far beyond Microsoft. He is a major investor, for instance, in enterprises as disparate as car dealerships and waste management. He is also the founder of Corbis, a vast picture archive that stands to make him a fortune as the demand for digital images rockets, and is a major shareholder in a social networking site for researchers, along with a think tank and a venture capital firm. However, there is still plenty of money to spend on other things.

As noted elsewhere, he has not always been keen to flash the cash. It certainly hasn't all gone on expensive restaurants. 'I eat McDonald's more than most people,' he told *Playboy* in 1994. 'In terms of fast food and deep understanding of the culture of fast food, I'm your man.' And in the same interview he explained his hitherto refusal to buy himself a plane: 'Why? Because you can get used to that kind of stuff, and I think that's bad. So I control that kind of thing intentionally. It's one of those discipline things. If my discipline ever broke down it would confuse me, too. So I try to prevent that.'

Yet by 1997, his self-imposed prohibition on private jets was over (even if his taste for junk food was not). That year he invested in a Bombardier BD700 Global Express jet, and was unlikely to have got much change out of $50 million. However, aircraft never did it for Gates like cars could. From even before he could drive, he was something of a piston-head. Driving became an outlet for him in the early days of Microsoft, a way to let off steam and break up the long hours and days devoted to coding. Nor was he interested in leisurely driving, but lusted after speed. In fact, he earned a succession of speeding tickets (even once getting one in a power boat) and on one occasion was arrested in Albuquerque after getting into a spat with a traffic cop.

SPLASH OUT ON YOUR PASSIONS

Gates has always been happy to channel some of his income into motor cars. Having owned an orange Mustang while still at school, he was willing to spend hundreds of thousands of dollars at a throw to get the latest in big boy's toys. One of his earliest purchases was a 1979 Porsche 911 that tore up the roads of New Mexico. Other Porches followed, including a 930 Turbo, a Carrera Cabriolet and a 959 Coupe, of which only 330 or so were ever built. However frugal he may have been in other areas of his life, when it came to cars, the rule book went out of the sunroof.

His brushes with driving and the law didn't stop there. One of his cars, the Porsche 959, prompted Gates to push for a change in American law. A noted supercar, the 959 is among the most advanced 'on-the-road' sports cars ever built (it has a top speed of 195 mph and can hit 60 mph in just over 3.5 seconds), but it was technically illegal in the US since its crash rating was unknown. Bill's car was thus kept in storage for a decade in the Port of Seattle by the US Customs

Service. However, Gates was one of several notable figures to lobby the White House for a reappraisal, and in 1999 President Bill Clinton amended legislation so that certain collectible cars were exempted from existing safety regulations. It has been reported that Gates had created a programme to simulate the vehicle's crashworthiness to drive the process forward. Other vehicles owned by Gates include a Ferrari 348 and a Jaguar XJ6, while he is also known to have driven a Lexus, a Mercedes and, more prosaically, a minivan.

Then there is his property portfolio, dominated by the Lake Washington estate that serves as the family's principal home. Built over approximately seven years from 1990 (often to the chagrin of wealthy neighbours unused to such wholescale disruption to their domestic setting), it has a footprint of over 6,000 square metres and is known as Xanadu 2.0, a nod to the property featured in Orson Welles's classic movie, *Citizen Kane* (which itself was based on William Randolph Hearst's castle at San Simeon).

With an interior created by the notable designer Thierry W. Despont, its features include twenty-four bathrooms, a garage large enough for twenty-three cars, a lake-view dining room that seats a hundred, a twenty-seat cinema, a devoted trampoline room with a twenty-foot-high ceiling, and its own boathouse.

Unsurprisingly, it is also filled with cutting-edge technology, a veritable experiment in state-of-the-art living. Famously, guests receive a PIN number on arrival that ensures that their stereos play their taste in music as they move from room to room, while high-definition screens display artworks pleasing to their particular eye. As of 2013, the property was estimated at $150 million. Gates's other properties include a mansion in Florida, complete with a showjumping arena, while there has long been a rumour, never confirmed, that he owns a private island off the coast of Belize in Central America.

He has also invested heavily (some experts believe paying over the odds) in classic works of American art. Indeed, it has been noted that Microsoft has directly and indirectly birthed so many billionaires who reside in Washington state that Seattle is destined to become a cultural capital, with treasures to rival the likes of Washington, D.C., New York and Boston. Gates's first significant foray into the art market came in 1996, when he paid $7 million for Andrew Wyeth's 1961 work, *Distant Thunder*. Two years later, he broke the record for a sum paid for an American artwork when he bought Winslow Homer's *Lost on the Grand Banks* (1898) for a cool $36 million. Other works in his private collection include William Merritt Chase's *The Nursery* (for which he paid $10 million), Frederick

Childe Hassam's *The Room of Flowers* ($20 million) and George Bellows's *Polo Crowd* ($28 million).

An avid collector of historic ephemera, he owns original documents in the hands of Isaac Newton and Abraham Lincoln. Then there is the extraordinary treasure that is Leonardo da Vinci's Codex Leicester. A seventy-two-page notebook dating from the first decade of the sixteenth century, it contains an array of thoughts and observations from Gates's hero on topics ranging from astronomy to fossils. He paid $30.8 million for it in 1994, causing uproar among Italians upset that it was departing their homeland. Gates, though, argued it was a document that reflects global cultural heritage. 'I remember going home one night and telling my wife Melinda that I was going to buy a notebook,' he would later wryly recall. 'She didn't think that was a very big deal.'

THE RICHEST MAN IN THE WORLD

'I wish I wasn't … There's nothing good that comes out of that.'

BILL GATES ON BEING THE WORLD'S RICHEST MAN, 2006

Since it first hit the shelves in 1917, *Forbes* magazine has been the bible of the super-rich, and in 1987 it began publishing an annual list of the world's billionaires. In 2015, Bill Gates retained his spot at the top of the tree, his fortune estimated at $79 billion. It was the second consecutive year he had been first place on the rich list, having been ranked second behind Mexican business magnate Carlos Slim between 2009 and 2013. In 2008 Gates had also been second, that time behind his old buddy Warren Buffet, but before that he had been in pole position every year since 1995.

By certain measures, there are historical figures who have boasted greater wealth than Gates. For instance, at his richest, the oil baron John D. Rockefeller had a fortune equivalent to 1.5 per cent of the USA's entire GDP at the time, while Gates's bank balance equated to a mere 0.4% of American GDP when measured in 2013. However, in dollar terms, no individual has ever been as rich as Gates at the time of writing.

As a youth, he is said to have vowed to become a millionaire by the time he was thirty. He actually reached that milestone several years ahead of schedule. He was only just over thirty (in fact, he was thirty-one) when he became a billionaire. That was in 1987, and came about as a result of the previous year's public flotation of Microsoft stock. Remarkably, it was a move about which Gates was very mixed. His inclination was that a company becomes harder to manage and more unwieldy when shareholders have the right to call the CEO on all of his big decisions. Furthermore, business was so buoyant that the company did not need a cash injection – often the prime reason for going public. But he also recognized that Microsoft had become far too big to stay as it was. Additionally, offering stock options was vital in order to attract and retain the most talented employees. Not only did it provide staff with a financial incentive to make the company as successful as possible, but it also gave employees a personal stake in the company, helping to bind them together.

Regardless of Gates's misgivings, the 1986 flotation ushered in the financial good times for the workforce. And for those with the patience to keep hold of their stockholdings, the rewards have been phenomenal. For instance, someone who invested $10,000 in 1986 would have found themselves with an investment worth $2.4 million in 1998. It is estimated that Microsoft's initial public offering created three billionaires and some 12,000 millionaires within a few months of trading.

Gates himself sold a relative handful of shares on the first day of trading, earning a mere $1.6 million. However, his remaining 45 per cent shareholding was valued at $350 million. Suddenly Gates was not merely a bright young thing in the tech business but one of the hundred wealthiest people in the richest country in the world. By 1987, his stake had tipped past the billion-dollar mark. Up and up it went, until by the late 1990s he was established as the richest man in the world – a status he has easily retained, even after being overtaken as Microsoft's biggest shareholder for the first time in 2014, by his successor as CEO, Steve Ballmer.

But being rich is not all that it's cracked up to be. According to G. Pascal Zachary in his book *Showstopper!*, Gates believes the rich don't 'get much credit for anything'. If anyone should know, it's Bill.

Take Time to Reboot

'I never took a day off in my twenties. Not one.'

BILL GATES QUOTED ON THE *MAIL* ONLINE, 2011

It almost goes without saying that Bill Gates has never been work-shy. Indeed, the young Gates who fell asleep in the middle of meetings and thought nothing of a thirty-six-hour shift was a veritable case study in workaholism. While he could hardly be accused of easing up in his later years, he has nonetheless developed a somewhat more measured approach to his personal workload.

As we have seen, from early in its growth, Microsoft had an intriguing and even contradictory philo-sophy in relation to mixing work and pleasure. On the one hand, there were the on-site leisure facilities provided for the workforce at not inconsiderable expense. On the other, there was the anecdotal evidence of employees expected to work impossibly long weeks that only the strongest survived for any length of time.

Gates was the personification of this contradiction. Against the marathon stints of coding, there were, for instance, the spontaneous jaunts across the New

Mexico desert in his car. He also kept up a host of hobbies. He has been a keen golfer, who in the early 2000s reportedly played off a mid-twenties handicap, as well as a respectable tennis player, swimmer, skater and skier (both on snow and water). In addition, he has devoted considerable energies into improving his bridge skills, although his mentor Buffett remains some distance ahead of him. Other interests include music, with the 1940s and 1950s providing much of his favourite material. Frank Sinatra is the subject of particular admiration. And, of course, he has been sure to spend as much time as possible with his family. (His children, incidentally, apparently playfully taunt him with the lyrics to Travie McCoy and Bruno Mars's 2010 hit 'Billionaire', with its lyrics 'I wanna be a billionaire so freakin' bad / Buy all the things I never had / I wanna be on the cover of *Forbes* magazine / Smiling next to Oprah and the Queen …')

All of that might sound like Gates has an excellent work–life balance. Certainly, he has always sought out at least a little downtime from the demands of his career. However, it is difficult to spot just exactly when he relaxes. The broad range of pastimes he undertakes is less symbolic of a life of leisure than an indication of his desire to cram as much as possible into his waking hours. He has historically been phenomenally adept at burning the candle at both ends without the flame ever extinguishing. But gradually he came to realize an adjustment was needed in his lifestyle – particularly given that his philanthropy has taken up more of his personal resources. Developing the theme in the 2011 quotation at the beginning of this section, he continued, '… I'm still fanatical, but now I'm a little less fanatical.'

MANAGE LIKE GATES

As Microsoft boomed from the early 1980s and its vast profits trickled down through the workforce, Gates knew he needed to think of smart ways to keep his best guys. Why would someone stay with the company for the long haul, working ungodly hours, if they had already earned more money than they knew what to do with? One of his answers was to offer extended sabbaticals, during which an employee had the opportunity to explore other interests, to travel, work in the community and – just maybe – even have a rest. It is a perk that shows Gates always understood there was life beyond Microsoft, even in the days when he rarely got a taste of it himself.

So it was that eventually, and to the surprise of many observers, Gates made the decision that he needed to take a step back. The process began in 2000 when he surrendered his position as CEO to Steve Ballmer (a handover both men admitted was difficult to manage). Instead he became the company's chief software architect. In theory, he was returning to his first love of computer engineering, although only the naïve believed he could entirely divorce himself from the bottom-line aspects of the business. Then, in mid-2006, it was announced that Gates was to retreat from his day-to-day position with the company in 2008 in order to concentrate on his foundation's activities. His last day as a full-timer came in June of 2008, thirty-three years after he had founded the company. However, several colleagues pointed out that Bill Gates's part-time equates to virtually anyone else's full-time. Finally, in 2014 he gave up the company chairmanship too – a role he had filled since 1981. However, this was retirement Gates-style. Just as the chairmanship passed out of his hands, so it was announced that he had agreed to serve as a technology adviser to Ballmer's successor as Microsoft CEO, Satya Nadella. 'I'm thrilled that Satya has asked me to step up,' said Gates, 'substantially increasing the time that I spend at the company.'

And so Gates remains as busy, if not busier, than ever, travelling the world to maximize the impact of his foundation's work and lending a steering hand to the firm that he built from nothing. By no measure could he be described as putting his feet up. Nonetheless, he has adjusted his commitments to reflect his new priorities and to ensure he maintains sufficient fuel in the tank as he enters his seventh decade. He wouldn't want to slow up too much, anyway. As he noted in 2008 in a considerable feat of understatement: 'I'm not a sit-on-the-beach type.'

Read Like
Bill Gates

'I really had a lot of dreams when I was a kid,
and I think a great deal of that grew out of
the fact that I had a chance to read a lot.'

BILL GATES

There is a commonly voiced, though widely disputed, fear that those generations brought up with personal computers and all the distractions they offer have turned their backs on traditional pastimes such as reading. Hearteningly, though, Gates is a prodigious consumer of literature of all types. On his personal blog (www.gatesnotes.com), he devotes a great deal of space to logging his own reading, often accompanied by insightful reviews. In recent times he has also issued at least one list of book recommendations a year.

His passion for reading started early, as he revealed to Janet Lowe in 1998 for her book *Bill Gates Speaks*: 'Growing up, my parents always encouraged us to read a lot and think for ourselves. They included us in discussions on everything from books to politics.' He eagerly consumed the Tarzan stories of Edgar Rice Burroughs as a boy, and also set himself the task of wading through the *World Book Encyclopaedia*, which ran to twenty volumes at the time. He gobbled up biographies too, exploring the lives of such notables as Franklin Delano Roosevelt and Napoleon Bonaparte. Meanwhile, as a child brought up with the moon landings and with a natural scientific bent anyway, he unsurprisingly developed a taste for popular science writing – both fiction and factual.

The reading bug never left him. Throughout his adulthood he has striven to give an hour a day over to it, and more at weekends. Nor does he restrict himself only to books, but reads a newspaper every day and several magazines each week, on the basis that they keep him informed on a broad spectrum of subjects from current affairs to the latest computing technology. Furthermore, in one of his columns for *The New York Times* back in 1996, he spoke of the 'think weeks' he takes a couple of times each year. During these breaks he stocks up on books 'and other materials my colleagues believe I should see to stay up to date', using the time to re-energize and re-evaluate.

His choice of books can best be described as eclectic. In his own words: 'I read a lot, but I don't always choose what's on the bestseller list.' While he is by no means averse to fiction (Graeme Simsion's smash hit *The Rosie Project* made it onto his bookshelf on his wife's recommendation), most of what he reads is non-fiction because 'I always want to learn more about how the world works'. In an admission that must lift the souls of parents and teachers everywhere, Gates attests that it is through reading that he best learns.

As well as seeking out titles that teach him something new, he is drawn by gripping stories, especially those centred around human ingenuity. In 2013, for instance, he highly praised Marc Levinson's *The Box: How the Shipping Container Made the World Smaller and the World Economy Bigger*. It is not, perhaps, a title that would win everyone over, but Gates loved it for the remarkable light it sheds on globalization, business and philanthropy.

Many of his book choices reflect his passion for addressing the great problems and crises that the world faces. So, for instance, he has read titles as disparate as Paul Farmer's *To Repair the World*, the hugely apt *How to Spend $50 Billion to Make the World a Better Place* (a collection of essays edited by Bjørn Lomborg on the ten biggest challenges facing the planet today), Jeffrey Sachs's *The End of Poverty*, Steven Levitt and Stephen Dubner's *Superfreakonomics* (according to Gates: 'One of my favourite things in the book is the debunking of many of the studies economists have done that they use as the basis for claiming that people are irrational in their choices.'), Leon Hesser's *The Man Who Fed the World* (a biography of Nobel Peace laureate and agricultural scientist Norman Borlaug) and Katherine Boo's heart-rending study of modern Indian slum life, *Behind the Beautiful Forevers*.

A man renowned for his ability to rapidly self-educate on subjects that fascinate him, he also has a taste for raw science. An all-time favourite is *Surely You're Joking, My Feynman!*, an account of some of the exploits of Gates's beloved Nobel Prize-winning scientist, Richard Feynman, including his encounters with Albert Einstein and Niels Bohr. The mid-seventies classic *The Selfish Gene* by Richard Dawkins also had a profound influence on him in its investigation of human evolution. Of particular relevance to Gates as he first got to grips with coding was the epic *The Art of Computer Programming* by Stanford professor emeritus Donald Knuth. Extending over several volumes, it is a notoriously dense work to get through and Gates read it over a period of months in twenty-page chunks. Writing in *The New York Times in* 1995, he said, 'If somebody is so brash that they think they know everything, Knuth will help them understand that the world is deep and complicated.'

Meanwhile, we know that in more recent times Gates's scientific reading has included both *Weather for Dummies* and *Physics for Dummies*, as well as Walter Gratzer's hard-core *Giant Molecules: From Nylon to Nanotubes* and Karl Sabbagh's *The Hair of the Dog and Other Scientific Surprises*. And among the popular biographies he has consumed is Walter Isaacson's profile of Steve Jobs, while Gates's love of tennis is reflected in his choices of *Pete Sampras: A Champion's Mind* and Andre Agassi's autobiography, *Open*.

In an interview with Achievment.org in 2010, he revealed his love of John Knowles's *A Separate Peace*, which he described as 'phenomenal'. Published in 1959, it is a coming-of-age novel set against the backdrop of the Second World War. Continuing the theme of American classics, he is a huge fan of F. Scott Fitzgerald's *The Great Gatsby*. He even has the following words from the end of the novel inscribed on the domed ceiling of his personal library (which is replete with at least 14,000 titles and two secret book cases): 'He had come a long way to this blue lawn, and his dream must have seemed so close that he could hardly fail to grasp it.'

Ever the 'do-er', Gates has not been content to be a mere reader either, but long ago became an author, too. His first work, *The Road Ahead*, was co-written with Nathan Myhrvold and journalist Peter Rinearson. An analysis of the rise of the personal computer and a rumination on the internet revolution then in its

A NOVEL PERSPECTIVE

The novel Gates most admires is J. D. Salinger's
The Catcher in the Rye, the 1951 tale of sixteen-year-
old Holden Caulfield that is now regarded as one of
the great American literary works. Gates commented,
'I didn't actually read *The Catcher in the Rye* until I
was thirteen, and ever since then I've said that's my
favourite book. It's very clever. It acknowledges
that young people are a little confused, but can be
smart about things and see things that adults don't
really see.' Looking at things differently was certainly
a trait Gates had shown growing up, something
that he carried into adulthood and can best
be seen in the way he attacked the early
computer software market.

infancy, it was a bestseller for which publishers Penguin
reportedly paid an advance of some $2.5 million. Gates
set aside about four months for the writing process,
which he found to be a genuine challenge that required
him to focus on his thought processes and refine his
conclusions. 'My admiration for people who write
books has increased now that I've done one myself,'
he would later say. Writers the world over gracefully
accepted the compliment even as they dreamed of an

advance amounting to just a small proportion of that which Gates had commanded. Undeterred by his first experience as an author, he wrote a second well-received book, *Business @ the Speed of Thought*, in 1999, looking at the relationship between commerce and technology.

All of which should go to allay the fears of those suspicious that computers and books can happily co-exist in a post-Microsoft universe. It is true that some of his innovations have helped birth generations filled with individuals happier to stare at a screen lost in a gritty urban shoot-'em-up or pretending to be a star exponent of a sport they have never mastered in real life, but Gates himself could not personally do more to promote the value of reading. However, even he – the owner of a spectacularly beautiful traditional library, remember – concedes that time might be running out for the visceral delight of holding a physical book in one's hands. 'Digital reading will completely take over,' he said in 2011. 'It's lightweight and it's fantastic for sharing. Over time it will take over.'

GATES'S FAVOURITE BUSINESS BOOK

> 'The best business book I've ever read.'
>
> BILL GATES ON JOHN BROOKS'S
> *BUSINESS ADVENTURES*

As a sometime writer on the subject of business himself, Gates made a curious declaration to *Playboy* in 1994. Discussing whether additional years spent studying at business school give an advantage to aspiring entrepreneurs, he gestured to the walls of his office. A leading light of a modern commercial tsunami, he exhorted, 'Let's look around these shelves and see if there are any business books. Oops. We didn't need any.'

There is no doubt much to be learned from the fact that the richest man in the world made his pile after turning his back on academic study and throwing himself into the nitty-gritty of the commercial world. Whatever the textbooks might have said, Gates rewrote the rules. His words to *Playboy* were those of a corporate young gun rapidly ascending the greasy pole of success on his own terms. Nonetheless, what he said was not altogether true.

The fact is, we *know* that Gates has read plenty of business books over the years, and has been happy to recommend several of them, too. For instance, he is a self-confessed fan of *The Ten Commandments for Business*

Failure by Donald R. Keough, who has inhabited the upper echelons of companies including Coca-Cola and Allen & Co. Drawing on over sixty years of experience, his book is described as a 'light-hearted "how-not-to" book'. Gates said of it: 'Don possesses a special combination of experience, wisdom, self-confidence and self-awareness. His commandments for failure will teach you more about business success than a whole shelf full of books.'

Other favourites include *My Years with General Motors* by Alfred Sloan, a 1963 work by the CEO of General Motors that is part memoir and part guide for aspiring tycoons. Gates once said of it: 'This is probably the best book to read if you want to read only one book about business.' And then there is Benjamin Graham's *The Intelligent Investor* (1949), the book that so influenced Warren Buffett and which Buffett in turn urged Gates to read.

But the volume that wins the greatest plaudits is another title to which Gates was directed by Buffett. There's nothing that will boost sales of your business book quite like the seal of approval from a bona fide global icon and the sometimes richest man on earth. When it turns out that another occasional richest man on the planet was the one who first commended it to him, you know you are on to a winner. That is what happened to a collection of John Brooks's articles published as *Business Adventures* back in 1969. Gates came across it when Warren Buffett presented him with an old copy after the two first met back in the early 1990s.

Sadly, Brooks died in 1993 and so did not reap the benefits of his book's renewed lease of life following an interview Gates gave in 2014 in which he praised the title. But he would surely have been heartened that there was still such an appetite for his work some forty-five years after it was first published. Having worked at *Time*, Brooks rose to fame as a columnist on the *New Yorker*, writing about business not merely to appeal to businessmen in suits but also to draw in the lay reader. The volume contains insightful essays on a wide range of subjects from the rise of Xerox to the lessons to be learned from the epic failure of the Ford Edsel motor car, via analysis of assorted corporate scandals. Gates said of it:

> Brooks's work is a great reminder that the rules for running a strong business and creating value haven't changed. For one thing, there's an essential human factor in every business endeavour. It doesn't matter if you have a perfect product, production plan and marketing pitch; you'll still need the right people to lead and implement those plans.

A lesson he learned well over his many years as Microsoft's main man.

Give
Something
Back

'In giving money, you have to be as careful as you are in making money. You want to make sure it goes to good causes. And so, if you just spend it in an unthinking way, it can be gone in a second.'

BILL GATES IN A 1998 INTERVIEW ON *20/20*

Gates's parents imbued their boy with a keen sense of civic and social responsibility, and his mother Mary gave up much of her time to voluntary work. Yet the reality of Gates's early career was that there was little scope for charitable works, although Microsoft as a corporation has long been involved in giving to charity, in the form of money, equipment and employees' time and expertise.

For a long while, Gates made little secret of the fact that his job as a software pioneer came first, and that 'good works' would have to wait. Take his words quoted in *Fortune* magazine back in 1987: 'I'm in a phase for the next ten years where my work is my primary contribution. The idea of funding other things is some time off.' Half a decade later, in 1992, he gave a journalist from the same publication a similar long-term outlook: 'Maybe ten years from now we'll be far enough along, and I'll put my head up and look around.' He essentially wanted the freedom to build a business empire without any distractions.

However, by the early- to mid-1990s, there was a definite shift in his approach. His public utterances on charitable giving reflected a new outward-looking Gates, as set against the one who had been entirely focused on growing his business. The first real statement of intent came in 1994 with the establishment of the William H. Gates Foundation – an initial step into the world of philanthropy, named after his father, who helped run the organization.

Its establishment was in no small part inspired by Mary Gates, who died that year after a fight with breast cancer. Her influence on her family and their commitment to giving something back was profound. Consider her son's words, delivered in a speech he made at Harvard in 2007:

My mother, who was filled with pride the day I was admitted here, never stopped pressing me to do more for others. A few days before my wedding, she hosted a bridal event, at which she read aloud a letter about marriage that she had written to Melinda. My mother was very ill with cancer at the time, but she saw one more opportunity to deliver her message, and at the close of the letter she said, 'From those to whom much is given, much is expected.'

That final sentiment was one that Gates himself almost replicated in 2006 when announcing his impending departure from his full-time role at Microsoft. On that occasion, he told the assembled journalists:

I believe that with great wealth comes great responsibility: a responsibility to give back to society, a responsibility to see that those resources are put to work in the best possible way to help those most in need.

However, if 1994 was the first major staging post in Gates's conversion into *philanthropist extraordinaire*, he was not yet ready to give himself fully to this new enterprise. In one of his *New York Times* columns the following year, for instance, he seemed to defer his transformation, while also pointing out the challenges he faced in knowing how best to use his wealth. 'Spending money intelligently is as difficult as earning it,' he said. 'Giving away money in meaningful ways will be a main preoccupation later in my life – assuming I still have a lot to give away.'

By 1996, though, his intentions seemed to be firming up as he began to utter a more consistent line. Again, it was via *The New York Times* that he revealed his thoughts: 'Eventually I'll return most of [my money] as contributions to causes I believe in, such as education and population stability.' The issue was forced a year later when media magnate Ted Turner received widespread publicity after giving a billion dollars of his personal fortune to the United Nations. After Turner challenged Gates and other members of the super-rich to do the same, Gates responded in an interview with Barbara Walters on the *20/20* show: 'Certainly, my giving will be in the same league as Ted's – and beyond.' It was a bold claim, but he had now committed himself.

Yet still there were some mixed messages. That same year, the *Forbes* publisher, Rich Karlgaard, noted Gates's reticence to throw his money at any old cause, saying, 'He has not squandered money on unworthy charities, despite enormous public pressure.' Meanwhile, a Gates comment concerning potential candidates as his successor at Microsoft hardly suggested much enthusiasm to pursue other avenues: 'Nobody is going to get me interested in some other job or activity, so it's very unlikely that we'd face that challenge.'

Nonetheless, 1997 saw the Gates Library Foundation give some $200 million in finance and the same again in Microsoft software to public libraries – more than the federal government managed that year. Regarding these venerable institutions as agencies of social equality, in which knowledge and access to information are vital currencies, he told *American*

Libraries magazine: 'Since I was a kid, libraries have played an important role in my life.' In fact, the book-lover and avid reader was now the biggest donor to libraries since Andrew Carnegie.

Yet, astonishingly, this now represents but a relatively minor footnote in the story of Gates's mission to give back some of that with which he has been blessed. As he ramped up his philanthropy in the 2000s, the public perception of Gates as an icon of American capitalist consumerism changed irrevocably. He summed up his dual existence to CNN in 2010:

I've been very lucky. I've had two jobs that were absolutely fantastic. When I was young, writing software, staying up all night, you know, dreaming about the personal computer I wanted and I thought would be great for everyone, that was the perfect thing for me. And now I've switched. I'm totally full-time on the foundation. You know, I'm loving advocating for these causes. I'm making sure that the money our foundation spends is used in the best way possible … I love doing this work.

Redefining Philanthropy

'If you believe that every life has equal value, [then] it's revolting to learn that some lives are seen as worth saving and others are not. We said to ourselves: "This can't be true, it deserves to be the priority of our giving."'

BILL GATES, COMMENCEMENT ADDRESS
AT HARVARD UNIVERSITY, 2007

Philanthropy is always a fluid concept, but ought to be understood as something distinct from charity. The word itself is Greek in origin and translates as 'the love of mankind'. But what differentiates philanthropy from charity? It is not merely scale, although philanthropists are generally dealing in very large sums of money, while a charitable donation can be simply a little loose change. Perhaps more helpful is to see charity as a way of alleviating the symptoms of a problem and philanthropy as a means to address its root causes. The difference, as it were, between giving a hungry man a fish to eat and giving him the equipment and expertise to catch fish himself.

America has a rich heritage of industrialists reinvesting their wealth to the greater good of society, with figures like Andrew Carnegie leaving extra-ordinary legacies. Gates himself has cited John D. Rockefeller as a particular inspiration. Rockefeller (1839-1937) made his fortune in oil but redirected a great part of it towards education, medicine and scientific research – an approach with obvious echoes in Gates's own work.

If there was a road to Damascus moment on Gates's philanthropic journey, it was a visit he made to Africa in 1993 – a safari in Zaire (now the Democratic Republic of Congo) – with his then soon-to-be wife, Melinda. Gates was, of course, a well-educated man who knew in abstract a little of the inequalities of the globe. But, confronted by extreme poverty at first-hand, his perceptions were fundamentally changed.

The struggle faced by millions of ordinary citizens was equally traumatizing for Melinda, who later told a journalist that after returning home she confided to a close friend: 'Africa changed me forever.' In the months that followed their return, Bill and Melinda educated themselves in some of the key issues. That millions of children were dying each year from diseases that no one died from in the USA had a particular impact. Within a year or two, Gates's focus was no longer homed in on Microsoft's well-being alone.

As he has become increasingly involved in phil-anthropic enterprises he has refined his guiding philosophy. Just as he exerts enormous control over what goes on in his commercial life, he likes to keep a tight hold of the strings in his philanthropic undertakings, too. He has referred to his particular brand of beneficence as 'catalytic philanthropy', filling a gap that he says exists between the private and public sectors.

That is not to say he underestimates the size of the task in hand. He understands that both private interests and national and supranational governmental organizations are key to resolving many, if not all, of the problems his foundation seeks to tackle. As a man who has played the capitalist game with the best of them and come out on top, it is perhaps no surprise that he retains enormous faith in the power of private capital. 'I am a true believer in the power of capitalism to improve lives,' he has said. Yet he is not blind to its shortcomings either. Writing for *Forbes* magazine in 2012, he observed:

> While the private sector does a phenomenal job meeting human needs among those who can pay, there are billions of people who have no way to express their needs in ways that matter to markets. And so they go without …

In the same article, he described how government 'can offer services where the market does not and thus provides a safety net'. In addition, some problems require resources to solve them that even a foundation as rich as Gates's cannot hope to provide alone. Additional billions from government budgets are essential. Nonetheless, he realizes that both private enterprise and government have limits to what they will invest in, with both fearing to overcommit to innovation. It is in this gap, he argues, that you may 'find a vast, unexplored space of innovation where the returns can be fantastic. This space is a fertile area for what I call catalytic philanthropy.'

As is to be expected, Gates is not afraid to take on the biggest challenges. Where once he set out to bring computers into every home, he is no less ambitious in his philanthropist guise. In a world where some 2.5 billion people live on less than $2 a day (a standard measure of poverty), and where income has such a direct correlation with health, mortality and educational opportunities, there is no shortage of problems to take on. As he and Melinda wrote on their foundation website, 'Warren Buffett once gave us some great advice about philanthropy: "Don't just go for safe projects," he said. "Take on the really tough problems."'

Characteristically, and crucially, Gates is prepared to weather some failures along the way. 'We not only accept that,' he has written, 'we expect it – because we think an essential role of philanthropy is to make bets on promising solutions that governments and businesses can't afford to make.' In his eyes, the role of the philanthropist is quite a simple one: it is to 'get things started'. 'For me it's proven the best job in the world,' he affirmed. 'As thrilling and humbling as anything I've ever done.' His approach is to altruistically address the gravest problems of our age with the same vigorous efficiency that he uses commercially. And it has changed the face of philanthropy for ever.

THE BILL AND MELINDA GATES FOUNDATION

'Our goals are focused on helping the poorest [globally] and improving education [in the US]. We spend half our money on global health.'

THE BILL AND MELINDA GATES
FOUNDATION WEBSITE

In 1994, Gates cashed in some of his Microsoft stock in order to establish the William H. Gates Foundation, named after his father who helped run it. For a while before, Gates Snr had been attempting to work through the grief of losing his wife by evaluating the masses of correspondence sent to his son requesting aid of one type or another. The foundation brought a deal more formality to this arrangement. Then, in 2000, Gates Jnr amalgamated this organization and his other philanthropic interests into the Bill and Melinda Gates Foundation. As of 2014, it was far and away the world's richest philanthropic institution, with over

$42 billion in assets. Moreover, it has set the standard for philanthropic practice in the new millennium.

At the centre of the foundation's work is an unshakable belief that every life has equal value. Bill's faith in equality among mankind owes much to his parents, and in 2008 he spoke on the *Charlie Rose* show about the enduring influence of his father on the way the organization is run: 'My dad has set an example by what he does ... he's the one who really got the foundation going, so my dad is somebody I aspire to live up to.'

In the words of its own website, the foundation hopes 'to help all people lead healthy, productive lives'. It teams up with an array of partners – governments, commercial enterprises and non-governmental bodies – in order to 'take on some tough challenges: extreme poverty and poor health in developing countries, and the failures of America's education system'. To this end, it is highly selective in the projects it adopts, focusing on those tackling the biggest barriers to people making the most of their lives. It also backs only ventures where it feels its contribution will make a material difference to its chances of success. It does not, therefore, contribute funds towards the fight against cancer on the basis that so much money is already filtered in that direction that any it adds would have minimal impact.

Given Gates's heritage, it is only to be expected

that the foundation has a particular interest in funding innovative and experimental approaches to problem-solving. For instance, it has invested in developing 'new techniques to help farmers in developing countries grow more food and earn more money; new tools to prevent and treat deadly diseases; new methods to help students and teachers in the classroom'.

With its headquarters in Seattle, the foundation operates satellite offices in Washington, D.C., Abuja (Nigeria), Addis Ababa (Ethiopia), Beijing (China), Delhi (India), Johannesburg (South Africa) and London (United Kingdom). There are four major grant-making programmes: a Global Development Programme, a Global Health Programme, Global Policy and Advocacy and a United States Programme. The latter scheme focuses on education provision while the international programmes seek to alleviate the problems of hunger and extreme poverty as well as striving to eradicate diseases (principally through mass vaccination programmes).

The foundation makes annual grants equivalent to about a tenth of the entire US aid budget. In 2006, Gates's friend (and a foundation trustee), Warren Buffett, swelled the coffers when he promised to donate shares in his Berkshire Hathaway business to a value of some $34 billion. Employing over 1,200 people, by September 2014 the foundation has disbursed a total of $31.6 billion in grants since it came into being, including $3.6 billion in 2013 alone, to projects in over a hundred countries worldwide. And bar a massive downturn in Gates's personal economic fortunes, the money should not dry up for a long time to come. It is his intention to give over 95 per cent of his wealth to the foundation, with the condition that it all be spent within twenty years of the death of either himself or Melinda (whichever is later).

Gates has insisted on the same vigorous approach towards the organization's activities as he demanded at Microsoft. But in return for the enormous energy he brings to the enterprise, he receives significant personal rewards. As he told *Businessweek* in 2009: 'I find the same magic elements that made me love my work at Microsoft ... I get to learn new things. But bringing top people together, taking risks, feeling like something very dramatic can come out of it – that's something that the previous work and the work now have in common.' The challenge of confronting a knotty problem, seeking a logical solution and overcoming widespread scepticism to implement it is a theme common to both his commercial and philanthropic activities.

As might be expected of any body imbued with so much influence, the foundation has its critics. There has been much scrutiny of its investments, with some accusing it, for instance, of supporting companies with poor environmental records and dubious commercial ethics. In particular, there have been claims, rejected by Gates, that money has been directed to pharmaceutical companies reluctant to supply their products to the developing world at a reasonable price.

He does, however, acknowledge that the odd misstep is inevitable. He and Melinda wrote in the foundation's annual newsletter in 2009: 'This lack of a natural feedback loop means that we as a foundation have to be even more careful in picking up our goals and being honest with ourselves when we are not achieving them.' And in the 2011 book *Reading with the Stars: A Celebration of Books and Libraries* (edited by Leonard Kniffel), he acknowledged, 'You know, in a lot of philanthropy, things don't go very well.' Nonetheless, the foundation has effected real change for good in its short life, from innovative library schemes within the United States to international vaccination programmes that have prevented hundreds of thousands, perhaps millions, of premature deaths.

Just as Gates came out of nowhere to become a serious player in the technology world, he has done exactly the same in the field of philanthropy. As Michael Edwards, an expert in the field, noted: 'The charity sector can almost disempower itself; be too gloomy about things … Gates offers more of a positive story. He is a role model for other philanthropists, and he is the biggest.'

Creative Capitalism

'How selfish soever man may be supposed, there are evidently some principles in his nature, which interest him in the fortunes of others, and render their happiness necessary to him, though he derives nothing from it except the pleasure of seeing it.'

ADAM SMITH, *THE WEALTH OF NATIONS*, 1776

In 2008, Bill Gates delivered a speech at the influential World Economic Forum held in Davos, Switzerland. In it he explained his theory of 'creative capitalism' as the best hope of successfully overcoming many of the challenges his foundation confronts. At its heart is the idea that the public, private and non-profit sectors work together (a significant departure from the classical model of American capitalism) to establish a system in which there are rewards for those who work to alleviate the world's ills. As he told his audience in Davos: 'This hybrid engine of self-interest and concern for others can serve a much wider circle of people than can be reached by self-interest or caring alone.'

It owes much to the theories of Adam Smith – one of the founding fathers of modern economics – and especially the ideas espoused in his landmark work, *The Wealth of Nations*. As Gates explained it:

Some people might object to this kind of market-based social change, arguing that if we combine sentiment with self-interest, we will not expand the reach of the market, but reduce it. Creative capitalism takes this interest in the fortunes of others and ties it to our interest in our own fortunes in ways that help advance both.

These were powerful words from such an icon of pure American capitalism – a man who built his business from scratch to become the richest person on the globe – and a self-confessed believer in the capitalist model. In Cynthia Crossen's 2000 work, *The Rich and How They Got That Way*, for instance, he was quoted thus: 'People underestimate how effective capitalism is at keeping even the most successful companies on edge.' So it was startling to hear him lay bare the shortcomings of the cash incentive as an agent of change that can alone combat all of society's problems. 'Profits are not always possible when business tries to serve the very poor,' he said. He suggested that the market can in fact drive social change, but not on a simple profit-motive basis; companies can reap benefits that might not be immediately financial. 'In such cases,' he continued, 'there needs to be another market-based incentive – and that incentive is recognition. Recognition enhances a company's reputation and appeals to customers; above all, it attracts good people to the organization.'

His commitment to 'creative capitalism' segues into the area of intellectual property, which has proved particularly controversial due to the vagueness of the lines separating the self-interest associated with capitalism and the pursuit of social good. His most rabid critics have gone as far as to accuse him of being part of some elaborate conspiracy by which the elite of the developed world keep developing nations in thrall to them by guarding their patents and expensively licensing life-saving drugs and crop-growing technologies. This sort of allegation may safely be filed under 'paranoia-fuelled'. Rather, Gates accepts that whatever the field – from his own software sector to pharmaceuticals and food grains – research and development is costly. As such, those who undertake it demand a return.

Although technological advances have improved the world for everyone (and Gates has enormous faith in the potential of biotechnology in particular to continue this upward swing), the extent and rate of improvement has been unequal. As he put it: 'The least needy see the most improvement, and the most needy see the least improvement, especially those that live on less than $1 a day.' He outlined part of the problem as follows:

When diseases affect both rich and poor countries, trickle down will eventually work for the poorest, because the high cost of development is recovered in the rich world, and then as they go off patent, they're sold for marginal cost to the poor and everybody benefits.

That is to say, the classical capitalist model ensures that the poorest benefit after everyone else. Gates's vision is that creative capitalism will help curb this unacceptable delay. His sense of urgency was evident to all: 'I am an optimist. But I am an impatient optimist.'

Bring Your
Celebrity to Bear

'I have to admit, I did not make it a priority.'

BILL GATES ON LEARNING OF BONO'S
DESIRE TO MEET HIM

Bill Gates has not traditionally been famed for his great personal charisma. John Lennon was once asked if Ringo Starr was the best drummer in the world, to which he supposedly replied that he was not even the best drummer in The Beatles. Given the spectre of Steve Jobs, it might similarly be said that Gates wasn't even the most charismatic of the cyber-geek CEOs. But, even if that is true, he has always confidently embraced his role as a public figure.

While he could never imbue a software launch with that sense of rock-and-roll anticipation that Jobs achieved, when it comes to talking about the world's really big challenges, he is lucid, considered and compelling. In the interests of his foundation's work he has eagerly tapped his own high profile, regularly taking advantage on an enviable contacts book and addressing the movers and shakers of the modern world on the biggest stages, such as at the United Nations.

It is not always clear how comfortable Gates is in courting celebrity, but wherever it can help him achieve his aims, he is content to do so. For starters, he knows that celebrity brings publicity and publicity brings influence. So he has used celebrity (his own and that of others) in order to advocate for the poor and unseen. For instance, in his 2011 annual letter – written as the international economy reeled from the impacts of a devastating slowdown – he said, 'The world's poorest will not be visiting government leaders to make their case, so I want to help make their case.'

Without doubt the most profound and influential 'celebrity hook-up' of Gates's life is his friendship with Warren Buffett. However, perhaps the most glamorous and headline-grabbing of recent times has been with Bono, lead singer of the band U2 and a long-time campaigner for a variety of causes, not least poverty and AIDS relief in Africa. Their joint 2005 *Time* 'Persons of the Year' accolade (also awarded to Melinda) is testament to the strength of their partnership.

On paper, it seems an unlikely alliance and, indeed, its genesis was not promising. Bono was the one who initiated proceedings. He already knew Paul Allen and asked for an introduction. When nothing immediately came of the request, the singer assumed it was Allen who was being evasive. In fact, Allen had made an approach and Gates had not been keen, believing Allen was talking about Cher's former husband, Sonny Bono.

However, when the pair eventually met, they immediately struck up a rapport. Gates recalled their first meeting: 'I was kind of amazed that he actually knew what he was talking about and had a real commitment to making things happen. It was phenomenal. After that, we've been big partners in crime.' Bono, meanwhile, has gone on record to say: 'I couldn't do anything that I do without the Gates Foundation.'

ONE LOVE

Gates assisted Bono with his ONE initiative ('an international campaigning and advocacy organization of more than 6 million people taking action to end extreme poverty and preventable disease, particularly in Africa') and RED campaign. This latter programme sees major international companies such as Converse, Armani and Gap co-brand with the campaign and donate a cut of their subsequent profits. It has succeeded in raising several hundred million dollars to purchase drugs for the treatment of AIDS sufferers. Who knew a rock-and-roll star and a computing genius would make such a potent team?

Gates has also significantly impacted on Bono's philanthropic methodology. Speaking to *Forbes* magazine in 2013 about his passion for drilling down into the facts and statistics of the problems facing the globe, he said:

> That's just me pretending to be Bill. I'm Irish; we do emotion very well. You're just experiencing some of it, and it can go on and on and on! I've learned just to be an evidence-based activist, to cut through the crap, find out what works and find out what doesn't work. I don't come from a hippie tradition of 'let's all hold hands and the world is going to be a better place'. My thing's much more punk rock. I enjoy the math, actually. The math is incredible!

But perhaps Gates's most important experiment in mixing celebrity and philanthropy will be the Giving Pledge, something he evolved along with Melinda and Buffett. Focusing on billionaires, it is an initiative that brings together both vast wealth and inevitably high public profiles. Its roots lie in Buffett's commitment to give away 99 per cent of his wealth to good causes and the Gates's own vow to do similar with 95 per cent-plus of theirs.

Those who sign up to the pledge – all billionaires or would-be billionaires were it not for their existing charitable giving – commit to giving away 50 per cent or more of their wealth to good causes. While it does not represent a legal contract, it is a moral commitment that few enter into lightly. Launched in relative secrecy at a dinner hosted by David Rockefeller on behalf of the Gateses at Rockefeller University in New York in 2009, the initial stellar guest list included businessman and former New York mayor Michael Bloomberg, Wall Street financier George Soros, Ted Turner (whose earlier challenge to Gates and his like was being returned to him with interest) and the multi-faceted Oprah Winfrey.

The campaign went public in 2010 and as of January 2015, there were reportedly 128 signatories to the pledge. Among them is Mark Zuckerberg, the founder of Facebook, who became a billionaire aged just twenty-three – a feat that makes Gates look like a positive slacker. Given the similarities in their career trajectories, Zuckerberg approached Gates about how best to undertake his own philanthropic projects. Gates happily adopted the role of mentor and it is another celebrity alliance that may yet reap extraordinary rewards for the wider world.

Philanthropic Aims: Providing Education and Equality of Opportunity

'Money has no utility to me beyond a certain point. Its utility is entirely in building an organization and getting the resources out to the poorest in the world.'

BILL GATES, *DAILY TELEGRAPH*, 2013

In a world where, to paraphrase George Orwell, some are more equal than others, it is telling that the wealthiest individual of us all is utterly appalled at the inequalities in resources and opportunity that divide our planet. His dedication to bridging these gaps shone through in the commencement address he delivered at Harvard University in 2007:

> Humanity's greatest advances are not in its discoveries, but in how those discoveries are applied to reduce inequity. Whether through democracy, strong public education, quality health care, or broad economic opportunity, reducing inequity is the highest human achievement.

This commitment manifests itself in several ways. His foundation, for instance, is a tireless campaigner for improving education about, and access to, family planning internationally. This, it believes, is a basic human right. Meanwhile, it strives to provide farmers in the developing world with the skills and tools to improve their efficiency and thus better profit from their labours. It is also a staunch supporter of the Alliance for Financial Inclusion, which aims to provide banking services to the vast numbers around the world who are currently unbanked. Through, for example, mobile-phone technology, it is hoped that financial services will become available to the world's poorest, enabling them to pay for essentials such as healthcare and generally to better manage their money.

All these initiatives are designed to lessen the natural disadvantages faced by those born in the developing world. But Gates is certain that education above all is key to levelling the playing field. Furthermore, he is intent that there should be equality of educational opportunity within the United States itself, independent of a student's financial or social background. So it is a source of frustration that the tale of his 'dropping out' of Harvard is so regularly retold. Writing in *The New York Times* in 1996, he said:

It concerns me to hear young people say they don't want to go to college because I didn't graduate. For one thing, I got a pretty good education even though I didn't stay long enough to get my degree. For another, the world is getting more competitive, specialized and complex each year, making a college education as critical today as a high school education was at one time.

When he was awarded an honorary degree by his alma mater, the irony was not lost on him: 'I've been waiting more than thirty years to say this: "Dad, I always told you I'd come back and get my degree."' As if to emphasize that he had actually been a committed student before leaving to pursue other opportunities, he added, 'I used to sit in on lots of classes I hadn't even signed up for.'

Allied to his faith in the power of education is his belief in the potential of youth to exploit it. With this in mind, as he asserted in another of his *New York Times* columns, he believes that children should be well schooled in the rudiments:

I'm one of those people who thinks kids ought to learn how to multiply with a pencil and paper even though calculators can do it for them. But at the same time, I have no doubt that computers can help kids develop more of their mental potential.

His personal experience as a young gun in the software business in the 1970s and 1980s convinced him that youth should be no barrier to achievement.

'When I was young, I didn't know any old people,' he told *Wired* in 2010. 'When we did the microprocessor revolution, there was nobody old, nobody.' He ruefully went on to note, 'It's weird how old this industry has become.' But his desire to give youth its wings is most neatly summed up in a remark he made to Michael Meyer in *Newsweek* in 1994: 'Young people are more willing to learn, [to] come up with new ideas.'

Gates is not blind to the opportunities he enjoyed as the result of being born into a relatively well-off family in twentieth-century America. 'I was a huge beneficiary of this country's willingness to take a risk on a young person,' he told an audience at Columbia University in 2009. Self-made as he was, he has never ignored the debt he owes to good fortune, and it is to be commended that he longs to extend the same opportunities to others.

Philanthropic Aims: Combating Disease

'A disease for which there is no effective therapy is an unsolved mystery.'

BILL GATES, *THE NEW YORK TIMES*, 1996

Opportunity, however, is worthless if one does not have the good health to take advantage of it. Therefore, the Gates Foundation's other great crusade is to fight disease – with a particular eye on those that besmirch the developing world but by comparison hardly register in the world's wealthiest nations. In 2005 he made the following mission statement:

> Global health is our lifelong commitment. Until we reduce the burden on the poor so that there is no real gap between us and them, that will always be our priority. I am not so foolish as to say that will happen. But that's our goal.

In order to have a chance of succeeding, he has got into bed with national governments, international organizations and pharmaceutical companies, staunchly defending the foundation against complicity in the incidental excesses of any of these other entities.

Furthermore, he takes a coolly rational approach to how the foundation spends its money, always taking into account the return on each investment – in other words, where his money is likely to have the greatest impact. If that sounds somewhat cold-blooded, it should also be remembered that it backs far riskier enterprises than many other charities (let alone governments) dare support when he and his fellow trustees are convinced they have a genuine shot at success. Its modus operandi was revealed in a statement from 2005: 'We have taken on the top twenty killers and for everything we do we look at the cost per life saved and real outcomes in terms of how things get improved.'

Malaria has been a natural target, given that it is a disease that almost exclusively impacts poor nations. Western Europe was rid of it by the end of the 1930s and it was considered eliminated in the USA in 1951, yet in 2012 there were some 2.7 million people afflicted with malaria, of whom 627,000 died. No less than 90 per cent of cases were in sub-Saharan Africa, with 77 per cent of sufferers aged under five. But the picture is not all bleak. Between 2000 and 2012 there was a 25 per cent decline in incidence and a 42 per cent fall in deaths, largely as a result of investment in diagnosis, treatment and prevention.

This is the sort of challenge – one with a virulent and devastating disease but also a real hope of making inroads against it – that the foundation is designed to take up. And it has done so with gusto, making around $2 billion in specific grants, as well as giving a further $1.6 billion to the Global Fund to Fight AIDS, Tuberculosis and Malaria. Indeed, AIDS is another one of the foundation's key battlegrounds. Despite its significant impact on the developed world, it is developing countries, and particularly those in sub-Saharan Africa, that have suffered disproportionately. For instance, in 2013 there were an estimated 35 million people living with HIV or AIDS, of whom 25 million were in that region. So it is that the Bill and Melinda Gates Foundation has made grants of $2.5 billion thus far in the ongoing fight.

However, the organization does not restrict itself to these 'big name' diseases, additionally running a bespoke programme to fight neglected infectious diseases. As of 2015, this scheme targeted eighteen neglected diseases affecting in the realm of a billion people. In each case, it is the foundation's belief that tactics including mass drug administration, public health surveillance and vector control (in other words, controlling the insects and worms that spread many of the diseases in question) can seriously reduce the incidence and impact of these ailments.

Among those conditions it has taken on are onchocerciasis (river blindness), a malady caused by a parasitic worm that is rarely mentioned in the Western press but which affects 18 million people each year, especially in Africa and South America. Other targeted diseases include dengue fever, Japanese encephalitis, human papillomavirus, visceral leishmaniasis (black fever), hookworm disease, dracunculiasis (guinea worm), lymphatic filariasis (elephantiasis) and human African trypanosomiasis (sleeping sickness).

From his youthful ambition to put a computer on every desk, the older Gates has adopted a far grander and selfless dream – to save the lives of millions of strangers.

THE FIGHT AGAINST POLIO

'You can actually take a disease and get rid of it altogether, like we are doing with polio.'

BILL GATES, *DAILY TELEGRAPH*, 2011

It is possible that Gates's greatest achievement will be to play a pivotal role in ridding the world of polio once and for all. In 1988 polio was endemic in about 125 countries, rendering 350,000 people paralysed each year, mostly children. That year saw the launch of the Global Polio Eradication Initiative, which championed an immunization scheme that has seen cases drop by an almost unbelievable 99 per cent. In 2012 there were fewer than a thousand new cases reported around the world, while there was a landmark announcement that India was polio-free – something many thought was an impossible aspiration. The disease today is endemic in only three countries: Afghanistan, Pakistan and Nigeria.

This achievement should not be underestimated. Only once before in human history has a disease infectious in humans been eradicated by purposeful intervention – the fate of smallpox in the 1970s. While many agencies have been instrumental in the fight against polio, the Gates Foundation has been among the most important. With the scent of complete eradication in his nostrils, in 2013 Gates announced plans to spend almost $2 billion over the following six years to see the job through.

It is a project that appeals to Gates's natural inclination for problem-solving, yet success is no foregone conclusion. For instance, in 2013 there were a spate of new cases in Somalia and war-torn Syria, where serious outbreaks would be hard to contain. Furthermore, Gates has faced political opposition to his endeavours, particularly in Pakistan where some Islamist groups have presented vaccination programmes as a Western plot to sterilize the indigenous population.

Nevertheless, Gates remains bullish about his

chances. In 2013 he told journalist Neil Tweedie: 'Polio's pretty special because once you get an eradication you no longer have to spend money on it; it's just there as a gift for the rest of time.' Nor does he intend stopping there, insisting, 'The great thing about finishing polio is that we'll have resources to get going on malaria and measles.'

Gates began his career seeking out bugs in computer programs. Polio, though, looks set to be the truly great bug-fix of his life.

Gates and God

'I'm a big believer in religious values.'

BILL GATES, SPEAKING ON *20/20*, 1998

Coming from a nation where espousing unconventional religious beliefs can cause you a great deal of grief, Gates has been somewhat guarded about his personal faith. Take his words from the *20/20* interview quoted above: 'I was raised religiously. And my wife and I definitely believe in raising our kids religiously ... As far as, you know, the deep questions about God, it's not something that I think I personally have the answers [to].'

As a child he attended the University Congregational United Church in Seattle, and we know that he memorized the Sermon on the Mount, although that was an incentivized achievement. He has also reported that he reads the Bibles customarily left in hotel rooms if there are no other texts to hand. However, none of this approaches testament to a profound religious belief. In fact, he made several statements in the 1990s that suggested fairly deep-seated religious scepticism owing to the lack of a concrete evidential basis (something he acknowledges is inherent in faith of any sort). So, for instance, in 1997 he told *Time*: 'Just in terms of allocation of time resources, religion is not very efficient. There's a lot more I could be doing on a Sunday morning.'

Yet there has always been a certain reluctance to rule out the possibility of a god altogether. When *Time* asked him if he believed in a deity, he responded, 'It's possible, you can never know that the universe exists only for me. If so, it's sure going well for me, I must admit.' Two years before, he had told David Frost: 'In terms of doing things, I take a fairly scientific approach to why things happen and how they happen. I don't know if there's a god or not, but I think religious principles are quite valid.' And in the same year he acknowledged a potential overlap between science and religion when telling Larry King: 'Even though I am not religious, the amazement and wonder I have about the human mind is closer to religious awe than dispassionate analysis.'

Then there is the influence of Melinda, who was brought up a Catholic and has remained within the faith even as her advocacy of family planning in the developing world has seen her lock horns with the Vatican. Meanwhile, in his 2013 interview with Neil Tweedie, Gates spoke of the need to sit down with the Pakistani authorities in order to negotiate the safety of those at the forefront of the polio vaccination programme, whom he described as 'women who are doing God's work'.

By the time he gave a wide-ranging interview to *Rolling Stone* magazine in 2014, he remained defiantly on the fence. He was, however, notably unwilling to completely dismiss the presence of a god in his life. For instance, he described the fight against global inequality in terms of a moral crusade and 'kind of a religious belief'. He also said, 'The moral systems of religion, I think, are super-important. We've raised our kids in a religious way.' And when explicitly asked if he believes in God, he said:

I agree with people like Richard Dawkins that mankind felt the need for creation myths … Now science has filled in some of the realm – not all – that religion used to fill. But the mystery and the beauty of the world is overwhelmingly amazing and there's no scientific explanation of how it came about … I think it makes sense to believe in God, but exactly what decision in your life you make differently because of it, I don't know.

As Gates approaches the later years of his life, he is perhaps less certain than ever as to whether there will be anyone to greet him once his time on earth has drawn to a close. He does, however, seem comfortable with the idea that religious faith provides a useful moral framework for those still toiling in this realm.

The Gates Legacy

'Legacy is a stupid thing. I don't want a legacy.'

BILL GATES, *DAILY MAIL*, 2011

It is perhaps modesty that causes Gates to insist he doesn't care how he is remembered, but it is a sentiment he has repeated on several occasions. For instance, he told the *Washington Post* in 1995: 'I don't have any particular goal for how I'm perceived. I've never written down how I want people to think about me.'

When pushed on the subject, he has sometimes resorted to self-deprecating humour, telling CNN in 2008: 'Who knows how history will think of me? You know, the person who played bridge with Warren Buffet, maybe. Or maybe not at all.' Meanwhile, he delivered the quotation at the start of this section in an interview with journalist Caroline Graham, before adding: 'If people look and see that childhood deaths dropped from nine million a year to four million because of our investment, then wow!' One suspects that the more mature Gates is less concerned with earning enduring personal fame than he is in leaving the world in a healthier state that when he arrived. The truth is, though, that he is on course to do both.

Although Gates's Microsoft career was indubitably driven – at least in part – by a hunger for acclaim and financial success, he has never been someone unduly concerned with what others think about him. After all, he himself has little time for reflecting on past successes, and he is also something of an iconoclast. Furthermore, his long life in the public eye has seen him become sceptical of the way one's life may be spun to fit someone else's agenda. As he told *Newsweek* in 1999:

> When somebody's successful, people leap to simple explanations that might make sense. So you get these myths. People love to have any little story. Yes, I'm intense. I'm energetic. I like to understand what our market position is. But then it gets turned into this – 'the ultra-competitor'. It's somewhat dehumanizing. I read that and say, 'I don't know that guy.'

Gates is one of that rare breed who genuinely appears to inhabit the present moment, though always with an eye cast to what he might achieve next. To dwell on what others might make of his efforts when he is no longer around would simply distract from the more important business of making the best of now. While he has been driven, focused and sometimes ruthless in pursuit of his goals, he has also been blessed with an inherent joie de vivre and optimism. As he put it in *The Road Ahead*: 'I think this is a wonderful time to be alive. There have never been so many opportunities to do things that were impossible before.'

It was a theme he touched upon two years later, in a 1997 column for *The New York Times*:

> Science fiction suggests that someday hundreds of people will fill a huge starship and spend generations traveling to a star … Maybe so, but I'm not getting on that ship! I'm sticking here. We have lakes. We have rivers. We have mountains. Earth is amazing compared to what's available in the surrounding few light years.

It is no doubt a good thing that legacy does not play upon his mind too much, since how the world remembers us once we're gone is one thing that none of us can control – not even Bill Gates. But as he transitions into the later stages of his life, it seems likely that history will look favourably upon him. He is by no means the first person to make a name and a fortune in commerce and then to create a second life as a philanthropist, but nobody has done it with as much panache for a hundred years or more. Evidence of the high esteem in which he is now held came in a poll conducted in early 2015 by YouGov for *The Times* newspaper. Almost 14,000 people from thirteen countries around the world were asked to name the person they most admired. Gates emerged as the clear winner, claiming a 10.1 per cent share of the vote, ahead of 9.3 per cent for Barack Obama. Nobody else polled more than 4 per cent.

As these final sentences are typed using Microsoft Word on a computer powered by Windows, it is difficult to remember a time when Gates's products did not influence our everyday lives. That his billions may yet extend and improve the quality of life for millions of the world's most deprived people is ample testament to a life well lived. That, surely, is legacy enough.

Selected Bibliography

Crossen, Cynthia, *The Rich and How They Got That Way: How the Wealthiest People of All Time – From Genghis Khan to Bill Gates – Made Their Fortunes*, Crown Business (2000)

Erickson, Jim and Wallace, James, *Hard Drive: Bill Gates and the Making of the Microsoft Empire*, John Wiley & Sons (1992)

Gates, Bill, *Business @ the Speed of Thought: Succeeding in the Digital Economy*, Penguin (1999)

Gates, Bill, *The Road Ahead*, Viking (1995)

www.gatesfoundation.org

www.gatesnotes.com

Ichbiah, Daniel and Knepper, Susan L., *Making of Microsoft: How Bill Gates and His Team Created the World's Most Successful Software Company*, Prima Publishing (1991)

Kinsley, Michael, *Creative Capitalism*, Simon & Schuster (2008)

Lammers, Susan (Ed.), *Programmers at Work*, Microsoft Press (1986)

Levy, Steven, *Hackers: Heroes of the Computer*, O'Reilly Media (2010)

Lowe, Janet, *Bill Gates Speaks: Insight from the World's Greatest Entrepreneur*, John Wiley & Sons (1998)

Manes, Stephen, *Gates: How Microsoft's Mogul Re-invented an Industry – And Made Himself the Richest Man in America*, Doubleday (1993)

Rogak, Lisa (Ed.), *Impatient Optimist: Bill Gates in His Own Words*, Hardie Grant Books (2012)

Slater, Robert, *Microsoft Rebooted: How Bill Gates and Steve Ballmer Reinvented Their Company*, Portfolio (2004)

Selected Bibliography

Stross, Randall E., *The Microsoft Way: The Real Story of How the Company Outsmarts its Competition*, Sphere (1998)

Zachary, G. Pascal, *Showstopper!: The Breakneck Race to Create Windows NT and the Next Generation at Microsoft*, Simon & Schuster (1994)

Get the whole *How to Think Like* series!

How to Think Like Einstein
978-1-78243-215-9
£12.99

How to Think Like Sherlock
978-1-84317-953-5
£9.99

How to Think Like Steve Jobs
978-1-78243-068-1
£12.99

How to Think Like Mandela
978-1-78243-214-2
£12.99

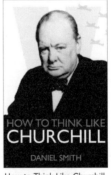

How to Think Like Churchill
978-1-78243-321-7
£12.99